THE TRUST CATALYST

Building Powerful Relationships to Skyrocket Your Sales

By:

Dean Thacker

Text Copyright 2024 – © Dean Thacker

All rights reserved worldwide. No part of this publication may be republished in any form or by any means, including photocopying, scanning, or otherwise, without prior written permission from the author.

Author's Note

Welcome to *The Trust Catalyst: Building Powerful Relationships to Skyrocket Your Sales*. Trust is a word that gets thrown around a lot, but when you really think about it, it serves as the foundation of everything we do in sales. It's the bedrock upon which long-term relationships are built, and without it, even the most promising sales opportunities can crumble.

When I look back on my own journey in sales, there's one thing that stands out above all else: every meaningful success I've had was rooted in trust. Whether it was the trust my clients placed in me to deliver on my promises or the trust I built over time through consistent, reliable interactions, I can honestly say that trust has been my greatest asset.

I remember a particular moment in my career that truly highlighted the power of trust. I had a client prepay me to detail their car for another day. I could've easily not shown up and kept the money, but instead, I showed up and did a great job on their car. The client was so happy and trusted me even more. Because of that trust, they spread the word about my business, and soon, I had three more clients because of them. That experience taught me that trust isn't just a tool—it's the cornerstone of every successful relationship.

This book is different because it doesn't just tell you what to do—it shows you how to build the kind of trust that transforms casual interactions into lasting relationships. You're not just going to learn about sales tactics or strategies; you're going to discover how to become the kind of person your clients can't help but trust.

Text Copyright 2024 – © Dean Thacker

All rights reserved worldwide. No part of this publication may be republished in any form or by any means, including photocopying, scanning, or otherwise, without prior written permission from the author.

Author's Note

Welcome to *The Trust Catalyst: Building Powerful Relationships to Skyrocket Your Sales*. Trust is a word that gets thrown around a lot, but when you really think about it, it serves as the foundation of everything we do in sales. It's the bedrock upon which long-term relationships are built, and without it, even the most promising sales opportunities can crumble.

When I look back on my own journey in sales, there's one thing that stands out above all else: every meaningful success I've had was rooted in trust. Whether it was the trust my clients placed in me to deliver on my promises or the trust I built over time through consistent, reliable interactions, I can honestly say that trust has been my greatest asset.

I remember a particular moment in my career that truly highlighted the power of trust. I had a client prepay me to detail their car for another day. I could've easily not shown up and kept the money, but instead, I showed up and did a great job on their car. The client was so happy and trusted me even more. Because of that trust, they spread the word about my business, and soon, I had three more clients because of them. That experience taught me that trust isn't just a tool—it's the cornerstone of every successful relationship.

This book is different because it doesn't just tell you what to do—it shows you how to build the kind of trust that transforms casual interactions into lasting relationships. You're not just going to learn about sales tactics or strategies; you're going to discover how to become the kind of person your clients can't help but trust.

As you turn these pages, you'll find practical advice, real-world examples, and actionable steps you can take right now to start building more trust in your sales process. But more than that, I want you to feel like we're having a conversation, like I'm right there with you, guiding you through each step. Because trust isn't just something you give; it's something you live.

I'd be remiss if I didn't take a moment to acknowledge the many people who have contributed to my understanding of trust in sales. First and foremost, I want to thank my father, Brandon Thacker. One of the most valuable lessons you taught me was the importance and value of trust—the same trust that you built your life upon. And to my mother, Crystal Thacker, who taught me how to love and care for others no matter what you're personally going through. Your compassion and resilience have been a guiding light, reminding me that trust is rooted not only in reliability but also in empathy.

Finally, to you, the reader—thank you for taking this journey with me. I'm excited to share what I've learned, and I'm confident that by the time you finish this book, you'll have a deeper understanding of the true power of trust in sales.

Table of Content

INTRODUCTION.. 10

CHAPTER 1: THE FOUNDATIONS OF TRUST...................... 15

How Trust Influences Buying Decisions..................................... 17

The Neuroscience of Trust in Sales... 19

The 5 Waves of Trust.. 23

Chapter Takeaways.. 27

CHAPTER 2: THE TRUST EQUATION..................................... 29

Components of the Trust Equation.. 29

The Role of Authenticity in Building Trust.................................. 34

Case Study: Brands That Exemplify Trust.................................. 36

Chapter Takeaways.. 37

CHAPTER 3: CREATING A TRUSTWORTHY IMAGE.............. 41

Developing Credibility... 42

Effective Communication and Transparency.............................. 42

Using Testimonials and Social Proof... 44

Chapter Takeaways.. 44

CHAPTER 4: THE ART OF ACTIVE LISTENING...................... 47

Techniques for Mastering Active Listening...47

Asking the Right Questions: Uncovering Customer Needs.........................50

The Real Power of Questions...52

Asking Questions Shows You Care...53

Demonstrating Empathy and Responsiveness..54

Chapter Takeaways..55

CHAPTER 5: CONSISTENCY AND RELIABILITY......................58

Maintaining Reliability in Customer Interactions.......................................59

Setting Clear Expectations..60

Managing and Raising Expectations..60

Chapter Takeaways...62

CHAPTER 6: TRUST-BASED SELLING TECHNIQUES............64

Strategies for Trust-Based Consultations...64

Personalizing the Sales Approach..66

Crafting Proposals That Resonate With Trust..69

Chapter Takeaways...71

CHAPTER 7: BUILDING LONG-TERM RELATIONSHIPS.......73

Personalizing Follow-Ups...75

Creating Value Beyond the Initial Sale..76

Chapter Takeaways..78

CHAPTER 8: THE ROLE OF EMOTIONAL INTELLIGENCE IN SALES 80

Enhancing Emotional Intelligence to Build Stronger Connections 81

Managing Your Own Emotions and Reactions 83

Reading and Responding to Customer Emotions Effectively 86

Chapter Takeaways 88

CHAPTER 9: NAVIGATING TRUST-BREAKING SITUATIONS 91

The Impact of Broken Trust 91

Identifying and Addressing Trust Issues 94

Learning from Trust-Related Failures 98

Chapter Takeaways 101

CHAPTER 10: THE ROLE OF SOCIAL MEDIA IN BUILDING TRUST 103

Engaging with Authenticity 106

Handling Negative Feedback Publicly 110

Chapter Takeaways 113

CHAPTER 11: BUILDING TRUST IN COMPETITIVE MARKETS 115

Differentiating Through Trust 115

Navigating Price Wars with Integrity 117

Trust as a Unique Selling Point...119

Chapter Takeaways..120

CHAPTER 12: LEVERAGING DATA AND ANALYTICS TO BUILD TRUST.. 123

Building Trust through Personalization...126

Chapter Takeaways..127

CHAPTER 13: TRUST BETWEEN SALES TEAMS AND INTERNAL STAKEHOLDERS.. 130

Internal Trust Building...130

Collaborative Selling..133

Maintaining Trust in Sales Leadership...135

Chapter Takeaways..137

CHAPTER 14: CULTURAL SENSITIVITY AND TRUST IN GLOBAL SALES.. 139

Understanding Cultural Norms..139

Adapting Communication Styles..144

Ethical Sales Practices in Global Markets..148

Chapter Takeaways..152

What's Coming Next?...155

CHAPTER 15: TRUST IN HIGH-STAKES SALES................... 156

Building Trust with High-Value Clients and C-Suite Executives....................156

Handling High-Risk Transactions 160

Trust When the Stakes Are High 161

Chapter Takeaways 163

CHAPTER 16: TRUST IN MARKET DISRUPTION 166

Building Trust Amid Industry Disruption 166

Transparency During Disruption 167

Resilience and Trust 168

Chapter Takeaways 169

CONCLUSION 172

Trust as a Unique Selling Point..119

Chapter Takeaways..120

CHAPTER 12: LEVERAGING DATA AND ANALYTICS TO BUILD TRUST..123

Building Trust through Personalization...126

Chapter Takeaways..127

CHAPTER 13: TRUST BETWEEN SALES TEAMS AND INTERNAL STAKEHOLDERS..130

Internal Trust Building...130

Collaborative Selling..133

Maintaining Trust in Sales Leadership..135

Chapter Takeaways..137

CHAPTER 14: CULTURAL SENSITIVITY AND TRUST IN GLOBAL SALES..139

Understanding Cultural Norms..139

Adapting Communication Styles..144

Ethical Sales Practices in Global Markets..148

Chapter Takeaways..152

What's Coming Next?..155

CHAPTER 15: TRUST IN HIGH-STAKES SALES....................156

Building Trust with High-Value Clients and C-Suite Executives....................156

Handling High-Risk Transactions..160

Trust When the Stakes Are High...161

Chapter Takeaways..163

CHAPTER 16: TRUST IN MARKET DISRUPTION..................166

Building Trust Amid Industry Disruption..166

Transparency During Disruption..167

Resilience and Trust..168

Chapter Takeaways..169

CONCLUSION... 172

Introduction

"Trust is the glue of life. It's the most essential ingredient in effective communication. It's the foundational principle that holds all relationships." — Stephen Covey.

You're offering a product you know is exceptional and could truly make a difference. After doing your research, you're confident it could significantly impact your client. But as you begin your presentation, you notice a flicker of doubt in their eyes—a subtle hesitation, perhaps a slight pause or a wary glance. What's missing? It's not the quality of your product; it's trust. Without trust, even the most compelling offer can fall flat. You might have all the facts, figures, and features lined up perfectly, but if the person across from you doesn't feel they can trust you, it's as if your words are bouncing off a wall.

Research shows that approximately 79% of customers would rather buy from someone they trust, even if the product isn't flawless. Trust becomes the key that unlocks the door to a sale. It's the deciding factor that transforms hesitation into a confident, "Yes, this is exactly what I need." Trust is not an add-on to your sales strategy; it's the foundation upon which successful relationships are built.

So, why is trust so important in sales? Honestly, even with the best product in the world, doubts will creep in if trust isn't part of the equation. In my experience, trust isn't about the product or service itself—it's about the entire experience you create for your client. When people trust you, they feel that they're in good hands, that you'll follow through on your promises, and that you genuinely care about their needs. It's more than delivering a pitch; it's creating a relationship where your client feels understood and valued.

Reflecting on your own experiences, when you've made a major purchase, what tipped the scales in favor of one option over another? More often than not, it was your trust in the person or company you were dealing with. I know for me, trust has always been the deciding factor. It's what makes me feel confident in my decision, knowing that even if things don't go perfectly, I'm dealing with someone who will stand by me. Having trust in someone also provides a feeling of comfort like no other. The comfort is very attractive, and when you're put in a comfortable situation, barriers tend to drop—and you know what that means. The sale becomes much easier.

And trust is not just about making a sale but building loyalty. It's the foundation that keeps clients coming back. I've seen this time and again in my own career. When clients know they can rely on you, they don't just buy once; they return, time after time, because they trust that you'll continue to deliver. That kind of reliability isn't easy to find, and when you offer it, it sets you apart.

But trust doesn't just keep the door open for repeat business—it also creates growth opportunities. Clients who trust you are more willing to explore other products or services you offer. They're buying more than what is on the table today but investing in a relationship that they believe will continue to bring value. I can't tell you how many times a simple upsell or cross-sell turned into a significant business opportunity, all because the foundation of trust was already there.

Over time, this trust leads to sustained business growth. The purpose of this book is to expand your view of selling from closing deals today to building a future with your clients. Clients who trust you are more likely to refer others, creating a cycle of positive word-of-mouth that money simply can't buy. Trust helps you build a client base and a community of advocates who believe in you and what you offer.

However, it's essential to recognize that not all sales situations are the same. There are times when transactional selling—focused on short-term gains—remains necessary. In certain industries, like retail outlets, quick-service environments such as gas stations and fast food, or even in automated sales processes, the opportunity to build deep, personalized relationships is limited. These scenarios are driven by the need for efficiency, speed, and convenience. The nature of the transaction doesn't often allow for the creation of rapport, personalization, or the chance to educate prospects in depth about the product or service.

When we talk about relationship selling, we're discussing a different approach altogether. This strategy is more than about closing a sale; it's about cultivating long-term relationships with your clients. It's about creating customer loyalty and growing a client base that continues to buy from you, time and time again.

To me, this shift towards relationship selling has always felt more aligned with how I want to do business. It's not just about the immediate return on investment—but the lifetime value of each client. When you focus on building relationships, you naturally increase your ROI because you're creating a bond that encourages customer retention.

And let's not underestimate the power of customer feedback. When you build trust and establish a relationship, clients feel more comfortable sharing their honest opinions. This feedback, both good and bad, is invaluable for continuous improvement and growth.

The sales landscape has really evolved, moving from a focus on quick, transactional selling to something much deeper. In the past, sales were often about making a quick deal and moving on. This transactional approach, common in industries where products are commoditized, focuses on immediate gains—get the sale, move to the next. But there's a downside. This method lacks depth and fails to build lasting connections. Sure, you might close the sale, but what happens next? There's no relationship, no loyalty, and often, no repeat business. It's a constant cycle of chasing the next opportunity, with little to show for it in the long run. Think of it this way: there are only so many potential customers available. By prioritizing relational selling, you create opportunities to maximize the sales potential with each customer, building deeper, long-term relationships that lead to repeat business and referrals.

Contrast this with a relationship-based approach, where the goal isn't just to make a sale, but to build a connection. Here, the focus is on nurturing relationships that lead to ongoing business. Clients become partners in your success. By investing in these relationships, you create a foundation that supports long-term growth.

This book is designed for anyone who wants to build something lasting in their sales career. If you're looking to move beyond quick wins and create meaningful relationships with your customers, you're in the right place. Whether you're a seasoned professional or someone just starting out, this book offers insights that can change the way you approach sales.

Throughout these pages, you'll discover strategies and practical steps to help you build, maintain, and use trust to increase your sales and create lasting relationships. You'll learn how to turn prospects into loyal clients, making trust your most valuable asset.

This isn't just about theory; it's about real-world application. I've seen firsthand how these principles play out in everyday sales interactions. The tools and techniques you'll find here are meant to be used, starting now. Trust isn't just something you build; it's something you live, day by day, in every interaction. And as you work through this book, remember that the skills you develop will serve you in every aspect of your life, not only in sales. Trust is universal, and mastering it will open doors you never knew existed.

So, as you begin this journey, stay open to learning, apply what resonates with you, and watch how your sales and relationships transform. You're about to unlock powerful tools that will elevate your sales career and enrich your personal interactions. Happy reading, and may the trust you build lead to endless possibilities.

Chapter 1: The Foundations of Trust

"People buy from those they trust. Trust is earned through authenticity."
— Rachel Botsman.

Trust is not just a buzzword in sales; it's the cornerstone of every successful relationship. When you walk into a room, ready to pitch your product or service, what's the first thing that comes to mind? You might think about the features you want to highlight or the benefits that will set you apart from the competition. But underneath all of that, there's something far more fundamental at play: the trust your prospect has—or doesn't have—in you.

Trust is the quiet confidence a prospect places in your character, capability, and reliability. It's not something you can see or touch, but its presence (or absence) is felt in every word, every gesture, and every interaction. I remember early in my career when I was eager to close deals, focusing solely on the product's features and benefits. But there were times when I could sense a hesitancy, a resistance that I couldn't quite understand. It wasn't until I began to focus on building trust—really showing my clients that I was there to help, not just to sell—that I started seeing a shift in how they responded to me.

Think about it: from the customer's perspective, you are the product. You're the embodiment of everything your brand stands for. If they sense even the slightest disconnect between what you're saying and what you truly believe, that trust begins to waver. And once it's gone, it's incredibly hard to regain.

Let's explore a scenario that illustrates just how crucial trust is. Imagine a businessman with a genuine treasure map—a map he knows leads to a cave containing **$2 million** worth of gold. This isn't some fantasy or scheme; the treasure is real, and the businessman has verified it. However, he doesn't have the time to go on the journey himself due to his demanding schedule, so he approaches a traveler with an offer. He proposes to sell the traveler this authentic map for the traveler's modest life savings—a small investment compared to the potential fortune it could bring.

The traveler examines the map—it's simple, with rough markings, and while the promise is enticing, doubt starts to set in. Despite the businessman's assurances and the allure of a $2 million treasure, the traveler hesitates and ultimately walks away, unwilling to take the risk. What went wrong? Even though the treasure was real, the traveler didn't trust the businessman. Without trust and credibility, the opportunity felt too risky, and the chance for both parties to gain was lost. This highlights how even the most valuable opportunities can slip away if trust isn't firmly established.

This story might seem extreme, but it's a situation we encounter all too often in sales. How many times have you offered something valuable, only to see the prospect hesitate and ultimately decline? It wasn't because they didn't need or want what you were offering —it was because they weren't sure if they could trust you. There wasn't enough evidence to them that what you were selling wasn't a scam or wouldn't ultimately lead them to a loss. And that's where the role of the salesperson shifts. You're not someone who pitches a product; you're a problem-solver who genuinely cares about helping your clients.

I've learned over the years that the best salespeople see themselves not just as sellers but as consultants. They understand that their primary role is to solve the needs of their prospects. But before you can solve any problems, you need to build that relationship—a relationship rooted in trust. If you haven't established that trust, your prospects will unlikely open up about their real challenges. Just as you wouldn't tell an untrusted stranger all your problems, a prospect won't freely share their needs or concerns with someone they don't trust.

When you take the time to build a strong relationship, you show your prospects that you genuinely care about helping them. And when they believe in your intentions, they're more willing to let you in, to tell you what's really going on. That's when you can step in and provide a solution that truly resonates, meeting their needs in a personalized and thoughtful way.

How Trust Influences Buying Decisions

Trust doesn't sit in the background; it actively shapes every decision your clients make. It's not simply about whether they will buy from you today but how they perceive you and your intentions in the long run. When trust is present, your clients feel understood. They recognize your there to genuinely address their needs and solve their problems, rather than only caring about a quick sale.

Consider this: how do you feel when you're dealing with someone who clearly has your best interests at heart? You're more likely to share your thoughts, to ask questions, and to engage in a meaningful dialogue. That's the power of trust. It opens up a space for honest communication, where clients feel safe expressing their concerns and expectations. This isn't just about making them feel good—it's about laying the groundwork for a relationship that goes beyond a single transaction.

A strong relationship, built on trust, creates a positive loop. When your clients trust you, they're more likely to refer you to others.

And those referrals are gold. They come with a built-in level of trust because someone else has already vouched for you. This word-of-mouth marketing is one of the most powerful tools you have, and it's driven by the trust you've established with your existing clients.

But trust does something else, too—it provides a buffer when things go wrong. Let's be real: everyone makes mistakes. Maybe an order is delayed, or a product doesn't perform as expected. In those moments, trust acts as a safety net. Clients who trust you are more likely to give you the benefit of the doubt. They believe in your commitment to making things right, and because of that, they're willing to forgive and move forward.

We all make mistakes, which can sometimes have significant consequences in sales. But here's the thing: when you've taken the time to build strong relationships with your clients, those relationships can act as a form of "insurance" when things go wrong. If you make a mistake that negatively affects a client, one who trusts you and knows your true intent—to help them—will be much more forgiving than a client you've just met or one with whom you haven't invested the effort to build a lasting relationship.

So, as you can see trust isn't just a nice-to-have; it's the glue that holds your client relationships together. It turns a simple transaction into a partnership, a one-time deal into a long-term relationship. And as you continue to build and reinforce that trust, you'll find that it not only strengthens your current relationships but also attracts new clients who are looking for someone they can believe in.

The Neuroscience of Trust in Sales

Your brain and your clients' brains are working behind the scenes in every interaction you have—especially in sales. Have you ever thought about what actually happens in the brain when you're building trust with someone? There's a complex interplay of signals and chemicals at work that determine whether your client feels like they can trust you or not. From the moment you start speaking, their brain is scanning your tone of voice, your facial expressions, even your body language, to decide if you're someone worth trusting. So, what if I told you that understanding how your client's brain works could dramatically improve your ability to build trust and close deals?

Trust, at its core, is a biological process. Think of how you've felt when you instantly trusted someone—there's a calmness, a sense of security, right? That's not a coincidence. One of the key players in this trust game is a hormone called oxytocin, often called the "trust molecule." This hormone is released during moments of bonding—whether it's between parents and children, close friends, or business partners. So, how can you trigger oxytocin in a business context? It's not as complicated as it sounds. Through small gestures like eye contact, a warm tone of voice, or a genuine smile, you're signaling to your client's brain that you're safe, approachable, and trustworthy. Their brain is wired to respond to these cues.

Let's explore how this plays out. Imagine you're sitting across the table from a potential client. Even before you've spoken about your product, their brain is picking up on subtle cues—how you're sitting, whether you seem relaxed or stressed, if your tone is calm and reassuring or hurried and anxious. All of these factors influence whether their brain will release oxytocin or send out warning signals. Think back to a time when you instinctively trusted someone during a meeting. Chances are, they weren't just saying all the right things; their body language, eye contact, and tone probably all felt aligned. That's the power of oxytocin at work —it makes people feel good about the interaction, and as a result, they're more likely to trust you.

But it doesn't stop at oxytocin. Trust also taps into another chemical in the brain—dopamine, the "feel-good" chemical that makes us feel rewarded. When you establish trust, the brain releases dopamine, which creates a sense of pleasure and satisfaction. Ever noticed how a trusted salesperson can make a client feel more excited about their purchase? That's dopamine being released, enhancing the customer's overall experience and making the decision feel right. On a biological level, trust makes doing business feel rewarding, which means clients are more likely to say yes.

Now, here's a crucial point: trust isn't just about building positive emotions; it's also about reducing negative ones. The brain's amygdala, which is responsible for processing fear and threats, plays a huge role in whether or not someone feels safe enough to trust you. If there's even a hint of uncertainty or insincerity, the amygdala kicks into gear, putting your client on high alert. They might not even realize it consciously, but their brain is saying, "Something feels off." This is why it's so important to be transparent and authentic in your dealings. When your client senses that you're being open about potential risks or challenges, it puts their brain at ease, reducing the activity in the amygdala and making them more open to trusting you.

Let's put this into perspective with an example. Imagine you're negotiating a high-stakes deal. Your client is nervous, and their brain is likely hyper-focused on any signs that something might go wrong. What do you do? Instead of glossing over potential problems, you address them head-on. You acknowledge the risks and discuss how you've prepared to handle them. This act of transparency triggers a calming response in the brain—it signals that you're trustworthy because you're not hiding anything. Have you ever had someone be so upfront with you that it made you feel instantly more comfortable? That's what's happening in your client's brain when you lead with honesty.

Another fascinating element of trust in sales is the concept of consistency. The brain craves predictability, and trust is often built when your actions consistently align with your words. The more reliable you are in your promises and follow-through, the more your client's brain will associate you with safety and reliability. But here's the kicker: if you break that consistency, even once, it can have a lasting impact on the neural pathways of trust. Just like it takes time to build those pathways, it takes even longer to rebuild them once they're broken.

Think back to a time when a trusted partner or colleague let you down. How long did it take for you to rebuild that trust, if ever? That's because your brain had formed a pattern—each successful interaction reinforced that trust. But one misstep, and the brain had to reassess everything. This is why, in sales, keeping your promises and maintaining transparency is vital. Every time you deliver on your word, you're reinforcing the neural circuits that associate you with trust.

And what about decision-making? Trust plays a massive role here, too. When your client trusts you, their brain uses less energy to make decisions. Why? Because trust simplifies the process. When trust is present, the brain doesn't need to waste cognitive resources on second-guessing your motives or rechecking facts—it can focus entirely on the benefits of what you're offering. This means quicker decisions, smoother negotiations, and more favorable outcomes for you as a salesperson.

Think of a time when you made a decision without hesitation because you trusted the person or company you were dealing with. You probably didn't spend hours weighing the pros and cons—you just went with your gut, right? That's because trust reduces the mental friction that usually accompanies decision-making. When your client's brain trusts you, it fast-tracks the decision process, leading to quicker sales.

So, how can you consistently tap into the neuroscience of trust to improve your sales outcomes? It all starts with self-awareness. Are you communicating in a way that triggers positive responses in your client's brain? Are you using body language, tone of voice, and facial expressions that convey warmth and reliability? Are you maintaining consistency in your actions and promises? These might seem like small details, but they're the very elements that your client's brain is processing—consciously and unconsciously—when deciding whether or not to trust you.

The neuroscience behind trust is about understanding both your client's brain and your own behavior as well. How you show up, communicate, and handle challenges all play a role in whether that crucial bond of trust is formed. Trust, after all, isn't built in a day. It's nurtured over time through every interaction, every promise kept, and every moment of transparency. And when you master that, you're not just closing sales—you're building lasting relationships rooted in trust.

The 5 Waves of Trust

I've always been a fan of Stephen M.R. Covey, and his work has greatly impacted how I think about trust, especially in business. One of the concepts that stuck with me the most is his "5 Waves of Trust" from *The Speed of Trust*. When I first read the book, I found myself reflecting on how these waves show up not only in sales, but in everyday life. It's powerful to see trust broken down into such clear layers, and as I dove into it (no pun intended), I realized how critical it is to apply these waves, both personally and professionally. Covey's approach taught me that trust doesn't happen overnight—it's built in stages, or "waves," and each one sets the foundation for the next.

Let me walk you through these waves, sharing some key insights I've learned along the way. You'll see how they build on each other, starting with self-trust and growing outward to trust on a global scale.

1. Self-Trust

It all starts with you. Before you can expect anyone else to trust you, you have to trust yourself. Covey calls this *self-trust*, and it's about developing your personal credibility. Think about it: if you don't believe in your own integrity or abilities, why should anyone else? This wave asks some tough questions: Do you act with integrity? Are you capable? Can you deliver results? Covey breaks this down into four "cores" of credibility—Integrity, Intent, Capabilities, and Results. When you strengthen these cores, you become someone others can count on. And I can tell you from experience, when you show up with that kind of self-assurance, people notice.

Key question: *Am I someone others can trust based on my integrity and performance?*

2. Relationship Trust

This wave is about how you interact with others. It goes much deeper than the words you say, but how consistently you follow through on your promises. Covey lays out 13 behaviors that help build trust in relationships, such as transparency, honesty, accountability, and respect. This hit home for me because I've seen firsthand how reliability—whether in friendships, family, or business—can build or break trust. People are watching, whether we realize it or not. Are you the person who says what you mean and does what you say? Over time, these behaviors compound, strengthening trust or eroding it if you're inconsistent.

For example, I once worked with a business partner who always followed up after our meetings, no matter how small the task. His consistency made me trust him deeply, knowing he'd never let things slip through the cracks. That level of reliability builds a foundation for lasting relationships.

Key question: *Do I behave in ways that build trust in my relationships with others?*

3. Organizational Trust

Now, let's expand this trust into organizations. Covey talks about how trust is built not just between individuals, but within teams and entire companies. When leadership aligns systems, processes, and values around transparency, accountability, and fairness, it fosters trust across the organization. I've seen organizations where trust was high

—everyone felt valued, communication was clear, and people wanted to contribute because they felt safe. But I've also seen the opposite, where leadership wasn't transparent and employees felt left out. In those cases, trust eroded quickly.

A real-world example: I remember a company I worked with that made a point of aligning its goals with its employees' personal development. It regularly checked in with staff, provided growth opportunities, and celebrated wins across the board. You could see how this alignment between company goals and individual aspirations led to a deep sense of trust and loyalty.

Key question: *Is my organization structured in a way that promotes trust and ethical behavior?*

4. Market Trust

Moving beyond the organization, we get to *market trust*. This is where your reputation comes into play. In today's market, where information travels fast, your brand's trustworthiness can make or break you. Have you ever had a friend recommend a brand so highly that you trusted it immediately, just based on their word? That's market trust in action. Customers want to know that your brand is reliable, ethical, and consistent with what it promises. Covey emphasizes that this kind of trust isn't about one transaction—it's focus building a reputation that stands the test of time.

Think about Apple or Amazon. These companies didn't just build products—they built trust. Their customers know that when they buy from them, they're getting quality, consistency, and reliability. That's the power of market trust—it turns customers into loyal advocates.

Key question: *Does my brand inspire trust and confidence in the marketplace?*

5. Societal Trust

The final wave is *societal trust*, which is about contributing to the greater good. It's how your organization or personal brand impacts society at large. In today's world people want companies to make a difference. Think about socially responsible brands, like Patagonia or TOMS. These companies don't just sell products; they contribute positively to society, which in turn builds a deep level of trust.

I once worked with a client who was passionate about giving back to the community. Their business wasn't solely about profits; it had a more expansive view of creating jobs, supporting local education programs, and ensuring ethical business practices. That approach built trust not just with their customers, but with the community as a whole.

When you show that you're committed to doing the right thing on a broader societal level, it creates trust that extends far beyond your individual transactions. It's about being a responsible, ethical player in the world.

Key question: *Does my organization contribute to societal trust by acting in socially responsible and ethical ways?*

These 5 Waves of Trust are a roadmap for building trust from the inside out—starting with yourself and radiating outward to your relationships, your organization, the marketplace, and even society at large. It's a powerful framework that shows how interconnected trust is at every level of life and business. When you nurture trust at each wave, you create a ripple effect that not only improves your relationships and business outcomes but also contributes to a more trustworthy and ethical society.

Chapter Takeaways

Your business cannot thrive without trust—it's the foundation of every relationship you build, every sale you make, and every opportunity you seize. Trust transforms a hesitant prospect into a loyal client, someone who will return to you again and again, not just because of what you sell, but because of who you are. It's the most valuable asset in your sales arsenal, and it's something that must be nurtured and protected at every turn.

Take a moment to reflect on how trust plays out in your interactions. Have you been focusing enough on building that foundation or rushing to close deals without laying the groundwork? Trust isn't built overnight, but with consistent effort and genuine care, it becomes the pillar that supports your entire business.

Here are some exercises to help you deepen the trust in your client relationships:

- Reflect on a recent client interaction. Did you make an effort to build trust, or were you more focused on closing the deal? How might things have gone differently if trust had been your priority?

- Identify the traits that make you trustworthy in the eyes of your clients. Are you consistently demonstrating these qualities in every interaction?

- Think back to a time when a lack of trust cost you a sale. What did you learn from that experience, and how can you ensure it doesn't happen again?

- Consider how you can position yourself as a consultant rather than a salesperson. What steps can you take to better understand and solve your clients' challenges?

- Make a list of potential pitfalls in your sales process that could undermine trust. How can you address these issues to maintain strong, trusting relationships with your clients?

As we move forward, let's explore how trust can be broken down into its essential components. The *"trust equation"* can give you clear insights into how trust works in every interaction. What elements make up trust, and how can you measure and strengthen them in your daily interactions? That's what we'll be uncovering next.

Chapter 2: The Trust Equation

"Trust is the currency of the future. Every transaction will be based on it." — Ginni Rometty.

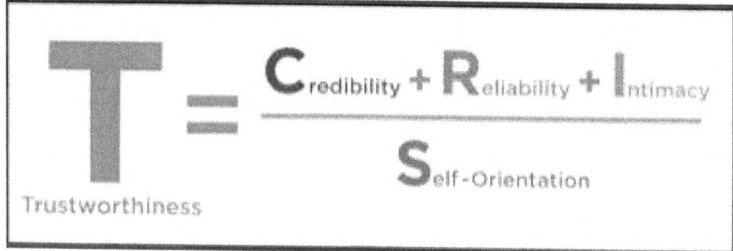

Trust like we have discussed is more than a desirable trait in sales—but a necessity. It underpins every successful interaction, every relationship that leads to repeat business, and every opportunity that turns into a long-term partnership. But trust isn't an abstract concept; you can *build, measure, and strengthen* it. This is where the **trust equation** comes into play. The trust equation provides a practical framework for understanding components that contribute to trust, giving you the tools to enhance this critical element in your relationships with clients.

Components of the Trust Equation

The trust equation comprises four key elements: **credibility, reliability, intimacy, and self-orientation.** Each plays a distinct role in building and maintaining trust, and when combined, they create a powerful foundation for any relationship. But how do these components come together in your daily interactions? Let's explore this further.

Credibility: Building Trust through Knowledgeable Communication:

Credibility forms the bedrock of trust. Your words are important, but the trust and reliability you convey make them truly impactful. When clients perceive you as credible, they're more likely to listen, believe, and eventually buy into what you're offering. But credibility doesn't come automatically—it's earned through knowledgeable communication and consistent behavior.

Think back to a time when you've trusted someone's advice. Why did you trust them? Was it because they spoke with authority, backed up their statements with facts, or perhaps because they seemed to really understand what they were talking about? That's credibility at work. It's the assurance that what you're hearing is not only true but also valuable.

For example, when a client says, *"I trust her insights on intellectual property because she is highly credible in that field,"* it reflects the trust that person has built through consistent, knowledgeable communication. But how do you build such credibility in your interactions? Many people think it's all about rambling off facts and details that you know about your product. The truth is, it's really about understanding your client's world—what challenges they face, what goals they're striving for, and how your solutions fit into that bigger picture. When you speak their language and address their specific needs with well-informed solutions, you become not just a salesperson—you become a trusted advisor.

Reliability: Demonstrating Dependability through Consistent Actions:

If credibility is what gets your clients to listen, reliability is what keeps them coming back. Reliability is all about following through—doing what you say you're going to do, every single time. It's about being that dependable person who clients know they can count on, regardless of the situation.

Imagine a scenario where you promise a client that their product will be delivered by tomorrow. If they say, "I trust him to deliver the product tomorrow because he has proven to be reliable," it's because you've consistently met their expectations in the past. Reliability goes beyond meeting deadlines; it's about showing up for your clients when they need you the most. Whether responding promptly to a concern or providing ongoing support after a sale, your reliability reassures your clients that they've made the right choice in trusting you.

Think about your own experiences—how does your reliability come across to your clients? Do they see you as someone who can be counted on, or are there areas where you could improve? Remember, reliability is built over time, but it can be damaged in an instant by a single broken promise. How can you ensure that you consistently deliver on your promises, reinforcing your clients' trust in you?

Intimacy: Creating a Safe Space for Clients to Share Their Needs:

Intimacy in the context of trust might not be what you first think of. It's not about personal closeness, but about creating an environment where your clients feel safe and secure in sharing their true needs, concerns, and even fears with you. When clients feel comfortable opening up to you, it allows for deeper, more meaningful interactions.

Have you ever had a client say, *"I feel secure sharing that information with her because she has always respected my confidentiality and would never embarrass me"?* That's intimacy at work. It's building a relationship where clients know they can be vulnerable, knowing that you'll respond with care, respect, and discretion. This level of trust enables you to get to the heart of what your clients really need, allowing you to offer solutions that are not only effective but also deeply personalized.

But how do you create this safe space? It starts with **active listening**—truly hearing what your clients are saying, without judgment or interruption. It's about being fully present in the conversation and showing that you value their input. How often do you make your clients feel heard and understood? Are you providing them with a space where they feel comfortable sharing their real concerns, or are they holding back because they don't feel that level of trust with you yet?

Self-Orientation: Focusing on the Client's Needs Over Personal Gain:

The final component of the trust equation is self-orientation, which asks the question: where is your focus—on yourself or on your client? High self-orientation can quickly erode trust, as clients may perceive you as more interested in your own gain than in their well-being. However, when you consistently put your client's needs first, it strengthens their trust in you and solidifies your relationship.

For example, if a client feels that *"I can't trust him on this deal because I feel he's more interested in his own gain rather than my interests,"* it's a clear sign that self-orientation is too high. On the other hand, when clients sense that you are genuinely concerned with their success and not just your own, they are far more likely to trust you. This means being willing to listen, to put their needs first, and to sometimes walk away from a deal if it's not in their best interest.

Reflect on your own approach: Are you truly focused on your clients' needs, or are you sometimes letting your own interests take precedence? Are you willing to walk away from a deal if it's not in the best interest of your client, even if it means a short-term loss for you? How can you shift your focus to ensure that your clients always feel like their needs come first?

Ultimately, the trust you build with your clients hinges on how well you balance these components. While you can't control how naturally trusting your clients are, you have complete control over your actions and words.

- Are you consistently building credibility by demonstrating expertise in your field? Are you reliable, following through on every promise?

- Do your clients feel safe enough with you to share their challenges, knowing you'll respond with empathy?

- And most importantly, do they feel that their needs are your top priority? When you bring these elements together, you create a bond that transcends the typical buyer-seller relationship, moving into a space of deep, mutual respect and trust.

A small tip: make it clear to your clients that you are open and happy to discuss any problems they might face. When clients know you're willing to address their concerns, they are more likely to engage with you openly and trustingly.

The Role of Authenticity in Building Trust

While the components of the trust equation provide a framework, authenticity is the thread that weaves them all together. Authenticity means being true to who you are—your personality, your values, and your character. It's the ability to interact with clients in a genuine and sincere way **without pretense or manipulation.**

In sales, authenticity often means standing out from the crowd. It's easy to follow a script and say what you think clients want to hear, but authenticity requires you to go beyond that. It's about showing up as yourself, with all your strengths and vulnerabilities, and connecting with clients on a human level.

Standing out can be uncomfortable. It puts you in a position where you're open to positive and negative judgment. But this is where the real magic happens. Daring to be yourself strengthens your relationships and opens you up to new opportunities.

Let me share an example that illustrates this beautifully. A young couple is looking to buy their first family car. Expecting a baby boy, they need something reliable. Their first stop is a dealership where they encounter a typical salesman. Distracted by thoughts of his upcoming vacation, he shows little interest in making a sale. The couple quickly realizes that he doesn't have their best interests at heart and moves on, feeling they won't find what they need with him.

At the next dealership, they meet a manipulative salesman who pressures them into considering a car they don't want. Feeling uneasy, they promptly leave, discouraged and tired.

Their last stop of the day brings them to you. Greeted with a warm smile and infectious enthusiasm, they explain their situation. You listen attentively, asking insightful questions to understand their needs better. The couple relaxes, sensing they are in good hands. You efficiently show them around the lot, highlighting a few suitable cars. Within 30 minutes, a sale is made, but not before you ensure they are completely satisfied with their choice.

Not only did the couple find the perfect car for their growing family, but they also became loyal customers. Over time, they referred four new prospects to your dealership. Your authenticity, genuine desire to solve their problem, and your enthusiasm made all the difference. This is the essence of good relationship selling.

Forming authentic relationships with customers is essential in sales. Customers value honesty and authenticity and can easily tell when someone is insincere or pretending. By being genuine, you instill confidence in prospects, making them see you as trustworthy. This authenticity encourages customers to engage with you and your brand, leading to stronger, long-term connections.

Case Study: Brands That Exemplify Trust

To truly understand the power of trust, let's look at a brand that has built its entire identity on it: "Nike". Nike is a sportswear company with a global symbol of trust, authenticity, and consistency. With annual revenues exceeding $50 billion, Nike has become the largest sportswear company in the world, and a significant part of its success comes from the trust it has built with consumers.

Nike's trust isn't just about their products—it's about what the brand stands for. Their slogan, "Just Do It," isn't just a catchy phrase; it's a call to action that resonates deeply with people around the world. Nike has built this trust through inspiring campaigns, community engagement, and a wide range of products that meet the needs of diverse consumers in various situations.

One of the most powerful symbols of this trust is the "Nike Swoosh". This simple logo has become synonymous with speed, progress, and victory. When people see the Nike Swoosh, they don't just see a brand—they feel a connection to Nike's values: *courage, power, and trust.*

As a salesperson, your name should become your own Nike Swoosh. When people hear your name, they should immediately think of credibility, reliability, and intimacy—just as we discussed in the trust equation. This is the level of trust you should aspire to build with your clients.

Chapter Takeaways

The trust equation is a practical tool you can use in every interaction with your clients. Trust doesn't happen by accident—it's something you build deliberately through credibility, reliability, intimacy, and a genuine focus on your client's needs. By embedding these elements into your everyday practices, you're not simply closing a deal—you're cultivating a relationship that can weather any storm and continue to thrive over time.

Reflect on your own journey. How often have you trusted someone because they consistently delivered on their promises? How did it feel when they took the time to truly understand your needs, making you feel that your interests were their top priority? These are the relationships that endure because they're built on a solid foundation of trust.

But let's not forget the importance of authenticity. Being authentic means being true to who you are, showing up honestly, even when it's tough, and always putting your client's needs ahead of your own. This is what turns a client into a loyal partner—someone who knows they can rely on you time and time again.

Now, to help you integrate these principles into your own sales approach, let's embark on a week-long self-reflection journey. Each day, you'll focus on a specific aspect of the trust equation, allowing you to internalize these principles and see how they influence your client interactions. By dedicating time each day to reflect on and apply these concepts, you'll start to notice subtle yet powerful shifts in how you engage with clients and how they respond to you.

Day 1: Credibility Check

Take time today to reflect on your credibility. How well do you know your product and the broader industry? Are you communicating this knowledge effectively to your clients? Make it a goal to deepen your understanding in areas where you feel less confident. Perhaps you could read up on recent industry developments or review case studies that highlight your product's strengths. How can you ensure that every interaction with a client demonstrates your expertise?

Day 2: Reliability Review

Today, focus on reliability. Consider your track record—do you consistently deliver on your promises? Think about a recent commitment you made to a client. Did you follow through? If not, what got in the way, and how can you prevent this from happening in the future? Set a personal goal to be impeccable with your word today, and notice how this impacts your client relationships.

Day 3: Building Intimacy

Your task today is to create a safe space for your clients. During your interactions, practice active listening without interrupting. How can you show your clients that you're genuinely interested in understanding their needs? Reflect on how often you invite your clients to share their concerns or challenges with you. What can you do to make them feel more comfortable opening up?

Day 4: Self-Orientation Awareness

Today, focus on where your attention lies during client interactions. Are you truly focused on their needs, or are you sometimes preoccupied with your own goals? Reflect on a time when you prioritized your interests over your client's. What was the outcome? How might things have gone differently if you had put their needs first? Challenge yourself to approach today's interactions with a client-first mentality.

Day 5: Authenticity Audit

Today, assess how authentic you are in your sales approach. Are there areas where you feel you're not being true to yourself? How can you align your actions more closely with your values? Consider a situation where being more genuine could have made a difference in your client relationship. What steps can you take to ensure that your interactions are as honest and transparent as possible?

Day 6: Client Feedback Collection

Today, reach out to a few clients and ask for feedback on how you're doing. This isn't about gathering testimonials—it's about understanding how your clients perceive your credibility, reliability, intimacy, and focus on their needs. What are you doing well, and where could you improve? Use this feedback to refine your approach and strengthen your client relationships.

Day 7: Reflect and Plan

On the final day of this week, take time to reflect on what you've learned. How has focusing on the trust equation impacted your interactions? What changes have you noticed in how your clients respond to you? Based on this week's insights, create an action plan for how you'll continue to build and maintain trust in the weeks and months ahead.

As you continue to apply these principles, imagine how much more successful your sales process could become if every client interaction was grounded in trust. Think about the impact this could have—not just on your current client relationships but on your overall career. What would it mean for your future if your name became synonymous with trust? The possibilities are endless, and it all starts with the foundation you've built in this chapter.

In our next discussion, we'll explore the practical aspects of building trust with customers, focusing on creating a trustworthy image that immediately sets the right tone in every client interaction.

Chapter 3: Creating a Trustworthy Image

"Your brand is what people say about you when you're not in the room."
— *Jeff Bezos.*

When people hear your name or see your brand, what do they think? The answer to that question can be the difference between a sale and a missed opportunity. We've all heard the old saying, "Don't judge a book by its cover," yet in reality, people do it all the time. First impressions stick. Before you even say a word, judgments are already forming, and in the fast-paced sales environment, those first impressions shape the way clients see you and your business.

Your trustworthy image goes beyond a well-dressed presentation or a professional handshake. It's how you communicate, the way you listen, and the reputation you build. Think about it like creating your own "Nike Swoosh." When people see that swoosh, they instantly think of reliability, consistency, and performance. You want your name to evoke the same feelings—credibility, transparency, and trustworthiness. But how do you go about crafting such an image?

Building a trustworthy image requires conscious effort and continuous action. From mastering product knowledge to effectively communicating with clients, you are always laying the groundwork for how people perceive you. Every interaction matters, and how you handle each one will either enhance or weaken your reputation.

Developing Credibility

Credibility is earned, not given. It's the foundation of trust and stems from how well you can demonstrate your knowledge and expertise. Clients need to believe that you are the go-to person in your field, and that belief is built when you speak with authority and confidence. But here's where many people get it wrong: they overwhelm prospects with endless facts and details. Sure, you might know your product inside out, but if you drown your clients in information, they'll switch off. Remember, it's not about showing off what you know but solving your client's problems.

Think about it like this: You wouldn't trust a doctor who gave you a complicated explanation of your symptoms without focusing on how to treat them. It's the same in sales. People don't buy products; they buy solutions to their problems. So, how do you use your product knowledge effectively? First, understand that clients ask questions not just to test you but because they need clarity. When you answer those questions confidently and creatively, your credibility naturally rises. Use your knowledge only to provide solutions.

Effective Communication and Transparency

We've all heard that communication is key, but there's so much more to it than just selecting the right words. Your tone, body language, and ability to actively listen all play crucial roles in delivering your message effectively. Imagine you're in a meeting with a client, and you need to communicate a serious matter—say, a delay in the project timeline. If you deliver this message in a casual, offhand tone, it's likely the client won't grasp the severity of the issue. They might even interpret your attitude as indifferent or unprofessional, leading them to feel frustrated or undervalued.

Conversely, if you use an overly dramatic or harsh tone, it can create unnecessary panic, making the client question your ability to manage the situation calmly and competently.

The way you speak often says more than the words themselves. A balanced, respectful tone that matches the seriousness of the situation shows that you're both attentive and responsible. It reassures the client that you're fully in control and committed to finding a solution. This approach helps avoid misinterpretation, ensuring your message is received as intended and reinforcing the trust and credibility you've built in the relationship.

The same goes for your body language. Non-verbal communication can speak volumes about your confidence, engagement, and intentions. Maintaining eye contact, nodding to show understanding, and keeping a calm posture are small actions that build rapport and trust with your clients. On the flip side, folding your arms, avoiding eye contact, or showing impatience can make your clients feel like they're not being heard.

Active listening plays a crucial role here too. When you're truly engaged with what your client is saying, you're showing that their concerns matter. This doesn't just mean hearing their words; it means picking up on subtle cues, understanding their body language, and responding in a way that shows you genuinely care. We'll dive deeper into this in the next discussion, but for now, understand that active listening is a powerful tool for creating meaningful, trustworthy connections.

Using Testimonials and Social Proof

In today's world, consumers rely heavily on the experiences of others when making decisions. Think about the last time you bought something online. Did you read the reviews? If you're like most people, you did, because we trust what others have experienced. This is why testimonials and social proof are incredibly valuable. They provide reassurance to new prospects that your product or service is tried and tested.

When clients see that others have already had a positive experience, the risk of doing business with you diminishes. Social proof is a powerful trust-building tool. It says, "If it worked for them, it can work for you too." A simple review or testimonial can transform a skeptical prospect into a confident client.

But here's where things get really interesting—testimonials do more than validate your credibility. They also create a sense of community around your brand. People want to be part of something, and when they see others benefiting from what you offer, they're more inclined to trust you and follow suit.

A study shows that 88% of consumers trust online reviews as much as personal recommendations. That's a huge number! But it also emphasizes how vital it is to consistently deliver exceptional service so that your clients leave glowing reviews. Remember, reviews are often the first step in building a relationship with a new client. They set the stage for the trust that will follow.

Chapter Takeaways

Creating a trustworthy image starts with the perceptions you leave behind and how those perceptions evolve over time. Trust isn't built overnight, and it's not something that you can manufacture with clever words or fancy marketing alone. It's grounded in your ability to demonstrate credibility through your knowledge, reliability through your actions, and intimacy through meaningful connections. When you back all of this up with social proof—genuine testimonials from satisfied clients—your image as a trustworthy, dependable professional becomes rock solid.

But it goes deeper than that. To truly master the art of trust-building, you need to align your intentions with your actions. Are you showing up authentically, or are you merely going through the motions? Your clients will notice the difference. A trustworthy image isn't just about how others see you; it's about how you consistently show up in every interaction.

Let's take a moment to reflect and consider how you can integrate these principles into your daily work. Here are some prompts to guide your thinking:

- When did you last use your product knowledge to help solve a client's problem? How did you ensure you didn't overwhelm them with information?

- How can you improve your communication with clients? Are you aware of how your tone and body language might impact your message?

- Think of a time when you failed to actively listen during a client interaction. What could you have done differently to make the client feel heard?

- How often do you request testimonials from satisfied clients? What can you do to encourage more reviews and build a stronger sense of community around your brand?

- What steps can you take to ensure that you consistently demonstrate transparency in all your dealings?

As we move forward, it's time to examine one of the most powerful tools in your sales toolkit: active listening. Speaking is only the first part to trust building communication. To be even more effective, it's important to understand the significance of listening- really listening-and responding in a way that meets your client's needs. Let's explore how mastering the art of active listening can transform your relationships and help you create even deeper connections with your clients.

Ask yourself: How would your business change if every conversation you had made your clients feel completely understood?

Chapter 4: The Art of Active Listening

"The most basic of all human needs is the need to understand and be understood. The best way to understand people is to listen to them." — Ralph G. Nichols.

Listening—it seems simple, doesn't it? Yet, in the fast-paced world of sales, where there's a constant rush to speak, persuade, and close deals, true listening often falls by the wayside. When we think of communication, we tend to focus on what we're saying, but the truth is, how well you listen is just as important. In fact, active listening transforms your conversations from mere exchanges into meaningful interactions that strengthen your relationship with the client.

Active listening isn't passive. It's engaging fully with the other person, not just hearing their words but also tuning into their feelings, thoughts, and concerns. It's the art of making your clients feel valued, showing them that their voice matters, and in turn, building trust. Think back to a time when someone truly listened to you—didn't it make you feel understood, like your thoughts and feelings were genuinely appreciated? That's what active listening does for your clients. It deepens your connection and lays the foundation for a long-lasting relationship.

Techniques for Mastering Active Listening

Active listening isn't completely about hearing words—it's also about truly connecting with the person in front of you. It involves three key components: **cognitive**, **emotional**, and **behavioral**. Together, they shape how well you understand your client and, more importantly, how much they feel understood. These elements create a conversation that is not only meaningful but builds the kind of trust that transforms interactions into long-term relationships.

Cognitive refers to the act of paying full attention and integrating information. It might seem straightforward, but how often are you in a conversation and your mind starts drifting toward what you're going to say next or how you'll respond? It's easy to get caught up in forming your reply or planning your next move, but true listening means slowing down and giving your undivided attention to the person in front of you. Real listening is not just about hearing the words; it's about absorbing the underlying messages—what are they really trying to convey? What emotions, concerns, or needs are behind what they're saying?

Imagine your client is explaining a challenge they're facing. It's tempting to jump in with a solution right away, but before you do, take a moment to really understand not only the surface problem but the deeper concerns that may be driving their frustration. They may be upset with more than the faulty product; they might be worried about how it's affecting their business, reputation, or even job security. Reflecting key points back to them is a simple yet powerful way to confirm that you've understood their core message. You don't need to parrot their words exactly, but by mirroring the essence of what they've said, you show that you're not only hearing them, but truly processing and valuing what they're sharing. If the client is new to you, this is one of the first ways to limit the self-orientation factor that we discussed in the trust equation. It shows that your genuine concern is helping them solve their problems. Their goals are now your goals. This creates a sense of trust that goes beyond just the exchange of words.

Emotional listening is about staying calm and compassionate in every interaction. Sales conversations can be emotionally charged

—there's excitement, pressure, and sometimes even frustration. However, one of the keys to active listening is keeping your own emotions in check. How often have you walked into a room and immediately picked up on someone else's stress or anxiety? Clients can sense when you're frazzled or rushed, even if you're doing your best to mask it. And that sense of unease can make them reluctant to fully engage or open up.

Think about how you would feel if you were meeting with a salesperson who seemed overwhelmed or impatient. You'd likely hold back, right? But when you remain calm, composed, and empathetic, it creates a safe space for your client to share their true concerns. Not only are you there to assist them in solving their problems-it is also your privilege to understand the client personally on a deeper level. Empathy is your most powerful tool here. When you put yourself in your client's shoes and see the situation from their perspective, you're not solely offering a solution; you're offering support. You're showing them that you care, that their success matters to you, and that you're willing to listen to their challenges with an open mind and heart.

Finally, there's the **behavioral** side of active listening, which is all about demonstrating your engagement through verbal and non-verbal cues. It's not enough to simply nod along or say "uh-huh" at the right moments. Your body language, tone of voice, and facial expressions all play a huge role in how well you communicate. Up to 90% of communication is non-verbal, so it's essential to be aware of what your actions are saying. Are you making eye contact, showing genuine interest, and leaning in slightly as the client speaks? These small gestures signal that you're fully present, fully engaged, and that you're taking their words seriously.

Pausing before you respond is another powerful behavioral technique. It shows that you're thoughtfully considering what they've said and aren't just waiting for your turn to speak. This simple pause gives the conversation a more reflective, thoughtful tone, allowing both you and your client to digest what's been shared. It also gives your client the opportunity to continue if they weren't quite finished—something that can deepen the conversation and strengthen your connection. One additional benefit of including pauses in your conversation, is its ability to provide you a moment to disconnect your responses from any emotional attachment you might have to them. Once again, keep away from expressing any thoughts or feelings that would likely deter your client.

Your clients are picking up on much more than your words— they're reading your entire presence. When they see that you're fully engaged both mentally and emotionally, the trust between you deepens. That's when true connection happens, and that's what leads to successful, lasting relationships. You're not just listening to make a sale; you're building a relationship based on mutual respect and understanding.

Asking the Right Questions: Uncovering Customer Needs

A vital part of active listening is asking the right questions. You might know your product or service inside and out, but unless you truly understand what your client is seeking, all that knowledge can fall flat. Think about it—how often have you been in a conversation where someone talks at you without really trying to understand what you're saying? It's frustrating, right? Now imagine being the client in that scenario. You don't only want to hear facts and figures; but you want to feel heard, and that's where asking the right questions comes into play.

Zig Ziglar, a renowned sales trainer, called this approach the "Needs Analysis." The idea is simple: asking questions to uncover your client's pain points, challenges, and motivations. But it's not about bombarding them with questions for the sake of it—it's about guiding the conversation in a way that helps both you and the client discover what's really at the heart of their decision-making.

Let's explore the different types of questions that can help you reveal what's truly important to your client:

- **Open-Ended Questions:** These questions give your client the space to express their thoughts and feelings without restriction. Instead of asking, "Do you like this product?" (which invites a yes or no answer), try asking, "What are your thoughts on how this product might meet your needs?" This opens up the conversation, allowing your client to share more than just a simple yes or no—they'll start telling you what they value, what worries them, and what they're excited about.

    Here's an example you might relate to: Imagine you're shopping for a new car. The salesperson asks, "What are your thoughts on the safety features?" instead of just, "Do you care about safety features?" Suddenly, you're thinking about your family, those long drives, and how much peace of mind a safer car would give you. You're no longer simply buying a vehicle anymore—you're making an emotional decision tied to your values. That's the power of an open-ended question.

- **Closed-Ended Questions:** These questions are more focused and are often used to clarify specific points. If a client mentions that they're concerned about pricing, asking something like, "Could you tell me more about what concerns you regarding the price?" invites them to expand on that particular issue. It keeps the conversation moving forward without making the client feel cornered.

A relatable example: Let's say you're considering hiring a freelancer for a project. The freelancer asks, "Can you share more about what makes you hesitant about the project cost?" Instead of shutting the conversation down with a simple yes or no, you're now engaging in a discussion about your budget, the scope of work, and your expectations. This level of clarity helps both parties get on the same page. The reason the closed ended questions are important is because it allows the sales person, in this case the freelancer, to dig deeper into the specifics of the client's concerns to better provide a solution that satisfies them.

- **Yes/No Questions:** While these questions can feel restrictive, they have their place in the conversation. Yes/no questions help you confirm details and make sure you're aligned with the client. For example, asking, "Would you agree that this solution addresses your main challenge?" helps you solidify where the client stands.

Picture this: You're speaking with a contractor about a home renovation project. After discussing your goals and concerns, they ask, "Would you agree that this design captures your vision?" A simple yes confirms that you're both in agreement, helping to ensure that the project moves forward smoothly.

The Real Power of Questions

When you ask the right questions, you're not just gathering information—you're demonstrating to your client that you genuinely care about their needs. You're showing that you're not just interested in making a sale but in offering a solution that truly fits their situation. Clients notice when you take the time to dig deeper, and it sets you apart from others who may just be going through the motions.

Let's take another example: You're sitting down with a client who is looking for new software for their business. Instead of asking surface-level questions like, "Do you like the interface?" you ask, "What's the most significant challenge your team is currently facing with your current software?" This type of question moves beyond the obvious and encourages the client to reflect on the pain points they might not have even fully considered. In doing so, you get to the heart of their issue and position yourself as someone who's there to provide real value.

Asking Questions Shows You Care

At the end of the day, asking the right questions is a powerful tactic that will lead you to success in sales, but it is less commonly but just as importantly known as a way to show your client that you care. When clients feel understood, they're more likely to trust you and, ultimately, to buy from you. It's not about manipulating the conversation to get what you want; it's about guiding the conversation to uncover what the client really needs. And when you do that successfully, both you and the client walk away feeling like the partnership was a win.

So, the next time you're in a conversation with a prospect, challenge yourself to move beyond the surface. Ask questions that uncover their deeper motivations. You'll be amazed at how much more meaningful your interactions become, and how much easier it is to provide solutions that genuinely resonate with your clients.

Demonstrating Empathy and Responsiveness

Beyond listening, your ability to show empathy and respond to your client's emotions is critical. Acknowledge their concerns, validate their feelings, and offer reassurance. When a client feels heard, they're far more likely to trust you and share openly. And trust is the foundation of any strong relationship.

Empathy is more than just understanding someone's words; it's about tuning in to their emotional experience. Imagine a client who's had a rough experience with a previous service provider. They might not say, "I'm frustrated," but their tone and body language speak volumes. This is where empathy becomes your superpower. You don't need to have all the answers immediately, but you do need to make them feel like their frustrations are valid. Saying something like, "It's completely understandable that you'd feel that way. I want to make sure this experience is different for you," shows that you're listening not only to what they're saying, but also to how they're feeling. It shows that their concerns matter and that you're committed to doing better.

For instance, if a client is hesitant to trust your solution because they've been burned before, it's easy to see how pushing for the sale would backfire. Instead, you could respond with something like, "I can see how that previous experience must have been really frustrating. My goal here is to make sure we find something that works for you, without repeating those mistakes." This goes beyond a sales tactic—it's a genuine human response. By addressing their emotions head-on, you're actively showing you're interest in making things better.

This approach also opens the door for them to share more openly. Often, when clients feel heard and understood, they become more willing to divulge the real concerns driving their hesitation. Maybe it's not just the product they're unsure of—maybe they've had financial setbacks or feel overwhelmed with choices. By creating a safe space for dialogue, you invite honesty and build a foundation for genuine solutions.

Finally, remember that empathy means being adaptable. Every client is different, and your approach should reflect that. For some, a quick conversation might be enough to build trust, while others might need more detailed explanations or even follow-up discussions to feel comfortable. One client may prefer a direct, no-nonsense approach, while another may need more hand-holding and reassurance. Whether it's adjusting your communication style to match their pace, taking extra time to understand their unique situation, or offering a tailored solution, showing flexibility builds deeper connections and creates lasting trust.

Take, for example, a client who needs extra time to make a decision. Instead of pushing them to commit on the spot, you could say, "I completely understand that this is a big decision for you. Why don't we take some time to ensure all your questions are answered, and we'll revisit it when you're ready?" This shows that you're focused on their needs, not just closing the deal.

Being empathetic and responsive isn't all about acknowledging emotions—it's taking meaningful action that demonstrates you're invested in their success, more than your own. That's how you build relationships that go beyond just a single sale.

Chapter Takeaways

The art of active listening goes far beyond hearing words—it's about creating a real connection, understanding needs, and responding with empathy. When you master active listening, you transform your interactions with clients from one-sided pitches to meaningful dialogues where your clients feel valued, understood, and supported. The trust you build through active listening is not just a stepping stone for a sale; it's the foundation of a long-term relationship.

Think about the power of asking the right questions. When you truly listen to your clients, you uncover their real pain points, and that's where the magic happens. Your solutions become more than just offerings—they become answers to their unique problems. By showing empathy, responding thoughtfully, and demonstrating genuine care, you create an experience beyond a simple transaction.

Now, let's take a moment to reflect on how you can bring these principles into your daily interactions:

- How can you improve your ability to focus fully on your clients during conversations? Are there distractions that are getting in the way?

- Think of a recent interaction where you could have asked better questions. What types of questions would have helped you uncover more about the client's needs?

- Reflect on your emotional responses during client conversations. How well do you manage your emotions, and how could this affect your client's trust in you?

- Are you using non-verbal cues effectively to show your clients that you're fully engaged? How can you improve this aspect of your communication?

- Think about the last time you demonstrated empathy in a client conversation. How did that interaction go, and what did you learn from it?

As we continue, think about the role consistency and reliability play in building trust. After all, listening is only one part of the equation—what you do with that information is what truly solidifies your relationship with your clients. Ask yourself, how reliable are you in delivering on the promises made through these conversations?

Chapter 5: Consistency and Reliability

"Consistency is the true foundation of trust. Either keep your promises or do not make them." — Roy T. Bennett.

Reliability is more than a trait; it's the foundation upon which trust is built. Think back to the Trust Equation we touched on earlier—reliability is a key component of that equation. Without it, the promises you make and the words you speak hold little weight. Reliability is more than showing up on time or doing what you said you would; it's creating a track record that clients can rely on without a second thought.

The best salespeople understand that trust isn't won in a day. It's earned through a series of small, consistent actions. To me, it's like putting deposits into a bank account. Every time you meet a deadline, follow through on a promise, or go the extra mile for a client, you're making a deposit. Over time, these deposits build into something incredibly valuable: trust. And trust, as you know, is the currency that keeps clients coming back.

I remember a time when I took on a client who was particularly hesitant. They had been burned in the past by salespeople who over-promised and under-delivered, leaving them feeling disillusioned. It took a while, but through consistent actions—delivering on every single promise and communicating clearly—they began to trust me. Eventually, that client not only stayed with me but referred me to several others. That's the power of reliability: it spreads beyond the immediate transaction and continues to pay off in the long term.

Maintaining Reliability in Customer Interactions

Reliability is a quality that has to be nurtured in every interaction. Your clients listen to what you have to say, but what's really important to them is that they know you will act upon your words. This doesn't only apply to big promises. It's in the small things too—the way you handle follow-up emails, how quickly you respond to questions, and how transparent you are about potential delays or challenges.

When customers invest in a product or service, they come with expectations. As Henrik Larsson Broman, a renowned sales expert and author on business strategy, says: "When your customers buy a product or service, they have certain expectations. They want to be sure they receive the promised benefits. They want the products and services to be delivered on time, and they want the expected result." Over-promising and under-delivering is a quick way to erode trust. In fact, it doesn't take many missed deadlines or forgotten promises before a client starts questioning whether they can rely on you at all.

I've found that the key to reliability is simplicity. Keep your word. It sounds so straightforward, but in practice, it's often forgotten. Think about it—how many people in your personal life do you trust implicitly because they always do what they say they will? The same applies in business. Some characteristics of a reliable person include being honest, keeping their word, maintaining consistency, safeguarding confidential information, and building a reputation that precedes them.

Setting Clear Expectations

When you think about your own role in sales, consider the expectations your clients have of you. Are they clear about what they can expect? This isn't just about product delivery dates or pricing. Customers expect you to communicate effectively, to provide honest information, and to be knowledgeable. They expect enthusiasm, positivity, and transparency. When you fail to meet these basic expectations, even if you deliver the product on time, trust can still be damaged.

To become the "Nike Swoosh" in your field—the recognizable symbol of reliability and quality—you must not only meet these expectations but exceed them. When people see the Nike logo, they have certain expectations about the quality and durability of the product. In the same way, your name should carry the weight of reliability. When clients interact with you, they should expect nothing less than excellence because that's the standard you've set for yourself.

Managing and Raising Expectations

The best salespeople don't stop at the expectations—they exceed them. The first step is setting those expectations clearly from the start, but the real magic happens when you find ways to go beyond what the client thought was possible. Every time you exceed a customer's expectations, you're delivering a product on a whole deeper level. A level where their trust is solidified in you. And trust, as we know, leads to loyalty.

I remember, when I was a child, some of the most exciting moments were when my parents surprised me with unexpected gifts or gestures. It wasn't about getting something on Christmas or my birthday; it was about those spontaneous moments—maybe a toy when I least expected it, ice cream for dinner, or even an unplanned family trip. What made these moments special wasn't the gift itself; it was the thought and care they showed when it wasn't expected. Those were the moments that meant the most and left a lasting impact on me.

Similarly, in sales, it's those unexpected, thoughtful gestures that truly stand out and build lasting trust with clients. I've seen this time and again. When you go beyond what's expected, even in small ways, clients notice. It might be an extra phone call just to check in, a personalized follow-up after a meeting, or sharing a helpful piece of advice when it's not anticipated. These actions transform you from a salesperson into a trusted partner in their journey. It's these moments of genuine care that elevate the entire relationship, making clients feel valued and understood.

Think about it like this: if you consistently exceed expectations, clients will begin to expect more from you. And while that might seem daunting, it actually creates a cycle of growth and improvement. Each time you raise the bar for yourself, you push yourself to become a better salesperson and professional. Exceeding expectations becomes a habit, and as it does, you'll find that your clients become more invested in you. They'll return again and again, not just because you provide a product or service, but because they trust you to always go the extra mile.

This doesn't mean you have to perform miracles overnight. It's about steady, incremental improvements. Over time, exceeding expectations becomes second nature, and that's when you truly start to see the benefits. Your clients will appreciate your dedication and want to tell others about their experience with you. This creates a ripple effect, leading to new opportunities, referrals, and a growing network of loyal customers.

And here's something I want you to think about: meeting expectations will keep you in the game, but exceeding them will set you apart. You want to be the person clients rave about and stand out because they consistently go above and beyond. It may not always be easy, but it is always worth it.

Chapter Takeaways

Consistency and reliability are the cornerstones of building long-term relationships. When you maintain reliability in every interaction, you show your clients that they can count on you—not once but every time. Reliability isn't all grand gestures but the small, daily actions that prove you're dependable. Whether it's meeting a deadline, following up on a promise, or going the extra mile, these actions build trust. Trust, in turn, deepens client relationships, making them more likely to return and refer others to you.

But beyond being reliable, it's rooted in setting expectations and then exceeding them. When you manage expectations effectively, you create a foundation for trust. And when you exceed those expectations, you take that trust to the next level. Over time, exceeding expectations becomes a habit—a natural part of how you do business. This habit doesn't just benefit your clients; it helps you grow both personally and professionally.

Exercises and Prompts:

1. Reflect on a recent customer interaction. Did you clearly set expectations from the start? How can you improve in managing those expectations moving forward?

2. Identify one area in your daily routine where you can improve reliability. Is there a habit you can develop to ensure that you're always following through on promises?

3. Think about how you can go above and beyond in a small way this week. Is there a customer you can check in with or a task you can complete ahead of schedule?

4. Review your client relationships. Are there any where expectations haven't been met? How can you rebuild trust in those situations?

5. Set a goal for yourself: how will you consistently exceed expectations in the next month? What steps can you take to ensure that you're not just meeting, but surpassing what's expected of you?

As you reflect on these ideas, consider the lasting impact of being someone clients can rely on. What if every client interaction you had resulted in not only trust but enthusiasm for the work you do together? This is where reliability truly shines—it transforms clients into advocates.

Next, we'll explore how you can leverage that trust to build stronger relationships and boost sales. You've laid the groundwork with consistency and reliability, now it's time to take those relationships to the next level with trust-based selling techniques.

Chapter 6: Trust-Based Selling Techniques

"The best salespeople know that their expertise can become their enemy in selling. At the moment of truth, they want to see the world through the customer's eyes." — Mike Bosworth.

One thing that consistently sets apart top-performing salespeople from the rest is their ability to build trust. The heart of trust-based selling isn't pushing products or services; it's positioning yourself as a partner, someone who sees beyond the sale to the deeper issues and needs of the client. To truly succeed in sales, you have to approach each interaction with the mindset that you are not just a salesperson but an advisor. And this means seeing the world through your customer's eyes—understanding their struggles, needs, and goals—and then helping them find the solution that fits best.

One of the most important lessons in my sales career is realizing that people don't want to be sold to—they want to feel understood. There was a time I was focused on showcasing my product's best features, but something was missing. Clients weren't connecting with me past the surface level. Once I shifted my focus from pushing products to really addressing their unique problems, that's when the relationships blossomed, and sales started coming naturally.

Strategies for Trust-Based Consultations

Sales is more than just offering a product or service to meet a need—it's about identifying and solving deeper problems and delivering real value. Think about the last time someone genuinely took the time to understand your needs. Didn't it make a world of difference in how you perceived their intentions? That's the difference between a transactional mindset and a consultative one. The most successful salespeople approach each interaction as an opportunity to build trust. They take on the role of a consultant, treating each prospect's situation with care, curiosity, and genuine interest. When you see yourself as a consultant rather than a salesperson, the dynamic changes. Instead of being seen as just another vendor, you become a trusted advisor—someone who can provide lasting value beyond just a one-time deal.

I remember when I first made this shift in my own career. There was a time I used to think that closing the deal as quickly as possible was the end goal. But over time, I realized something important: when I slowed down, truly listened to my clients' concerns, and started thinking like a problem solver instead of a seller, not only did I close more deals, but I built long-term relationships. This approach made my clients feel valued because they saw that I was genuinely invested in their success, not just in the sale.

At the heart of this strategy is authenticity. Authenticity is the cornerstone of trust-based selling. We've all been on the receiving end of a scripted sales pitch, and you can sense it instantly, right? There's something about those interactions that feels flat, disconnected, and at times, even manipulative. Clients can easily sense when you're just going through the motions or when you're saying what you think they want to hear. On the other hand, when you show up as your true self, without pretense or gimmicks, something powerful happens. You create a bond that lasts because clients appreciate realness. They want to work with people who understand them, not just sell to them.

Authenticity is about building a connection that transcends the moment. When you're authentic in your approach, you forge bonds that stand the test of time. You're not just creating a momentary connection but building a relationship that can withstand challenges. Your clients are more likely to take your advice, believe in your solutions, and come back to you again and again. Why? Because they trust you. And trust, once established, is incredibly powerful. It's what turns a one-time client into a lifelong partner.

Let me share another personal experience. There was a time I tried impressing a client by rattling off technical jargon and showcasing my knowledge. While I thought I was doing great, I could tell I was losing them. It wasn't until I took a step back, dropped the pretense, and focused on understanding their actual needs that things began to change. By simply being myself—listening, understanding, and offering thoughtful solutions—I ended up not only closing the deal but building a relationship that continues to this day. It wasn't about the perfect pitch; it was the genuine connection we made.

When you position yourself as a consultant, backed by authentic intent, clients start to see you differently. They see more than merely someone who wants their business—they see someone who is genuinely interested in their success.

Personalizing the Sales Approach

Personalization goes beyond addressing someone by their name or sending an email that mentions their company. It's making every interaction feel uniquely crafted for the individual you're working with. In today's sales environment, where prospects are constantly bombarded with generic pitches, true personalization can make all the difference. The key is to genuinely understand the person you're speaking with and make them feel like they truly matter.

Research consistently backs this up. When customers feel like they're being treated as individuals, rather than just another lead, they are far more likely to engage with you. Studies show that 90% of consumers find personalized experiences appealing, and 80% are more inclined to do business with a company that offers this level of care. It's easy to see why. Think about how you feel when you walk into a store and someone greets you by name, or when you receive a special offer tailored to your past purchases. It feels good, doesn't it? That's the power of personalization—it makes people feel seen and valued.

But true personalization goes beyond knowing someone's name or title. The essence lies in understanding what truly matters to them. When you take the time to uncover the details that go deeper—like their specific pain points, challenges, and personal preferences—you're building a connection that resonates. And when people feel valued, trust naturally follows.

So, how can you apply this in your own approach? Let's break it down.

Your first opportunity for personalization happens the moment you make contact with a prospect. Pay close attention from the start—ask thoughtful questions, observe their body language or tone, and really listen to what they're saying. If you learn their name early in the conversation, use it naturally throughout. Studies have shown that hearing one's own name can trigger feelings of recognition and importance, making them more comfortable and engaged.

Think back to a time when you were a customer, and someone made you feel like you were their only priority. How did that impact your experience? That's what personalization should feel like for your clients. When they sense that you are truly focused on them, it strengthens the bond between you. But personalization doesn't stop with the first interaction—it's an ongoing process. Every follow-up call, email, or meeting should build on the information you've already gathered. This continuous effort shows that you care about their specific situation, not just about making a sale.

Another essential part of personalization is building rapport. When you match the energy of your prospect—whether it's their tone, pace, or even their mood—you create an immediate sense of connection. This is a subtle but powerful way to help them feel more comfortable with you. If they're calm and measured, match that energy; if they're excited and upbeat, bring that same enthusiasm into the conversation. Building rapport isn't all about tone, though—it's noticing the little details that matter. Genuine compliments on their watch, their knowledge, or their style can go a long way in establishing a deeper connection.

For example, when you take a moment to acknowledge something as simple as their attention to detail, it shows that you're paying attention, and that can be incredibly meaningful. These small gestures can make someone feel seen as a person, not just a client. And when people feel that connection, they're much more likely to trust you.

Ultimately, personalization is about forming genuine partnerships. Each interaction you have with a client should make them feel like they are more than just another prospect—they're someone whose needs you are truly invested in meeting. When you approach sales with this mindset, you build trust far beyond a single transaction. You're laying the foundation for long-term, meaningful relationships.

Crafting Proposals That Resonate With Trust

You can step up trust in your game while creating the sales proposal. By the time your client sees your proposal, they should already trust you to a significant degree, but the proposal is what seals the deal. Here's how to ensure that your proposal not only resonates but also inspires confidence in your client:

- **Social Proof**:
Incorporate testimonials and positive reviews that showcase how you've helped others solve similar problems. When clients see that others have had a positive experience working with you, it reinforces their belief that they can trust you. Imagine a client hesitating about committing to a new software solution. Including a testimonial from a similar company that saw a 30% increase in efficiency after using your software would help alleviate doubts. Testimonials act like silent endorsements, offering reassurance that you can deliver on your promises. Doing this shows that your success is repeatable, not a one-time occurrence.

- **Client-Specific Solutions**:
Your proposal should feel like it was written specifically for your client, addressing their unique challenges and needs. Avoid cookie-cutter solutions that don't take their specific situation into account. For example, if you're proposing a marketing strategy, use the information you've gathered about the client's business goals to highlight exactly how your approach will help them achieve those targets. Personalization is key here. When the client sees their pain points acknowledged and your solution tailored to fit,

they'll feel understood and valued, increasing the likelihood of moving forward.

- **Realistic Timelines**:
Setting realistic timelines is key to maintaining trust—something we've touched on before. One of the most common mistakes is overpromising to close a deal quickly. It might seem like the right move in the moment, but when deadlines aren't met, it often leads to disappointment and a strain on the relationship. Instead, think about offering timelines that are not only achievable but also allow for a bit of flexibility. For instance, if you're managing a project, provide a timeframe that comfortably meets the client's expectations while giving yourself some buffer for unexpected hiccups. This way, if you deliver in 2 weeks when you promised 3, you'll exceed expectations and strengthen the client's trust in your reliability. On the flip side, missing a deadline can damage your credibility and impact the relationship you've worked hard to build.

- **Transparent Pricing**:
Clients value transparency, especially when it comes to money. Break down your pricing so the client knows exactly what they are paying for and why. For example, if you're offering a marketing campaign, instead of quoting a lump sum, itemize the costs—ad spend, creative development, analytics, etc. This way, clients can see the full picture and understand the value behind the cost. Transparent pricing removes the ambiguity and helps prevent price objections down the road. When you're upfront about costs, it signals to the client that you have nothing to hide, further building trust.

- **Flawless Presentation**:
  Your proposal is a reflection of your professionalism. A single typo or formatting error can undermine the trust you've built up to that point. Take the time to thoroughly review the proposal before submitting it. Ensure it's formatted cleanly, free from errors, and easy to read. Consider the impression a client might get from a well-polished, professional document versus one with careless mistakes. A flawless presentation shows attention to detail and respect for the client's business, further boosting their confidence in your ability to deliver.

Chapter Takeaways

Trust-based selling is not about fancy techniques or manipulative tactics—it's about genuine connection and solving real problems. To succeed in this approach, you need to see the world through your client's eyes, treat them as individuals, and tailor your solutions to meet their specific needs. Personalization is the cornerstone of this method. It's what sets you apart from others who are still stuck in the mindset of mass-selling techniques. And don't forget—your proposal is an extension of the trust you've already built. Ensure it reflects your commitment to transparency, reliability, and understanding of their unique situation.

Let's put this into action with some reflective exercises and prompts:

- Review your current approach to selling. Are you positioning yourself as an advisor, or are you pushing products? Reflect on how you can shift to a more consultative approach that solves problems rather than just selling.

- Practice personalization by researching your next client before your first meeting. What insights can you gather that will help you build rapport quickly?

- Take the time to craft a more personalized follow-up email for a recent client. Did you acknowledge their specific needs? How can you make them feel valued?

- Revisit a proposal you've recently sent. Were you transparent with your pricing and timelines? Did you provide social proof to help build trust?

- Challenge yourself to identify areas where you can improve your presentation skills. Is your grammar and formatting flawless? Are you communicating clearly and professionally?

As we wrap up this chapter, let's shift our focus to something deeper—the art of building long-term relationships. Trust doesn't end after the sale; it's something that needs to be nurtured over time. What would it mean for your business if every client became a repeat customer, someone who advocates for you because they trust you completely? We'll explore that next.

Chapter 7: Building Long-Term Relationships

"There is only one boss. The customer. And he can fire everybody in the company from the chairman on down, simply by spending his money somewhere else." — Sam Walton.

A sale isn't the finish line; it's just the beginning of a long-term relationship. In sales, your success is determined not by a single transaction but by the relationships you cultivate over time. When clients feel valued, appreciated, and understood, they will return again and again. Think about how you feel when you engage with a business that knows you by name, remembers your preferences, and follows up to ensure you're satisfied. It transforms a simple transaction into a meaningful, lasting connection. The key to thriving in any sales environment is to build these kinds of relationships, where loyalty isn't assumed—it's earned.

Strategies for Ongoing Engagement and Follow-Up

The follow-up is one of the most underrated yet powerful tools in your sales toolbox. A staggering 80% of sales require at least five follow-ups to close the deal, and yet, so many salespeople drop the ball after the initial conversation. To build long-term relationships, you need to stay on your client's radar without being overbearing. Follow-ups allow you to show that you care beyond just the sale, strengthening the trust between you and your client. Let's break down how you can use follow-ups to enhance your client relationships and keep the momentum going:

- **Frequency**: The key to successful follow-up is consistency, but it's important to strike the right balance. Clients appreciate persistence when it feels genuine, not when it feels pushy. Think of follow-up frequency like watering a plant: you want to nurture it enough to grow, but overdoing it can cause damage. Since research shows that 80% of sales require at least five follow-ups, staying in regular contact shows that you value the relationship. Whether it's a quick email or a more personal touch, your consistent engagement speaks volumes about your commitment.

- **Timing**: The optimal time to follow up is immediately after the last interaction—whether it's later that day or the next. A timely follow-up shows your attentiveness and helps maintain the momentum from the previous conversation. It's an opportunity to recap key points and offer any clarifications. This not only strengthens the understanding between you and the client but also opens the door for addressing any questions that may have arisen after the initial meeting.

- **Methods**: Emails are standard, but varying your follow-up methods adds a personal touch that can make a lasting impression. A handwritten note, a thoughtful gift, or even connecting on LinkedIn can make your follow-up feel more tailored to the client. Ask them their preferred way of staying in touch, which shows respect for their time and communication preferences. Using the right follow-up method further personalizes the interaction and makes your client feel valued.

Each of these elements plays a crucial role in ensuring that your follow-up efforts are both effective and relationship-driven. When done right, your follow-ups reinforce the trust you've already built and create more opportunities for ongoing engagement.

Personalizing Follow-Ups

Following up is a brilliant opening for personalization. A generic follow-up message can do more harm than good, as it shows you didn't pay attention to the details of your last interaction. I remember a time early in my sales career when I sent out a follow-up email that was clearly a copy-paste job. The client didn't respond, and when I later re-read the email, I could see why. It lacked any acknowledgment of their specific needs. Personalizing your follow-ups shows that you care and were listening.

When you reference what was discussed previously, it's a reminder that you're not treating them like just another number. Let's say they mentioned a particular challenge they're facing, like a tight budget or the need for a quick solution. Bringing that up in your follow-up shows them that their words weren't lost on you. This is what will set you apart. By finding ways that genuinely support your client's goals and overcome their challenges, you will complete the order and cement the relationship with them. That simple reference to their unique situation can also be the key to deepening the trust you've already built.

The tone of your message matters, too. Personalization isn't all facts and figures. On a deeper level, it's about empathy. Maybe during your conversation, the client mentioned being hesitant because they're concerned about their budget, or they're unsure if now is the right time to move forward. Instead of brushing that aside, address it head-on. You might say something like, "I understand your concerns about the budget, and I've thought of a few flexible options that might work for you." When you show empathy and acknowledge their feelings, you're reinforcing that you're in this together, not just looking to close a deal.

Consistency is another pillar of trust-building in follow-ups. The follow-up process includes way more than that one-time outreach after a meeting or sale. Staying connected with clients regularly—

whether it's checking in to see how they're doing, offering valuable insights, or simply staying top of mind—shows that your relationship doesn't end once the deal is sealed. I've seen countless examples of clients sticking with companies simply because they didn't disappear after the transaction. That steady presence keeps the door open for future opportunities, whether that's an upsell, a referral, or even just keeping your name in their thoughts the next time they have a need. When you personalize your follow-ups, show empathy, and remain consistent in your interactions, you create a lasting connection that extends well beyond the initial sale.

Creating Value Beyond the Initial Sale

Building lasting relationships go beyond making the sale; it's important to consistently show your clients that they made the right decision by choosing you. Post-sale follow-ups are the most effective ways to reinforce this trust. How often do you check in with clients after they've purchased your product or service? Not only are post-sale follow-ups a courtesy; they're an opportunity to ensure satisfaction, address any potential issues, and leave a lasting impression of care and commitment. Let's break down some key ways you can create value beyond that initial transaction:

- **Gathering Feedback**:
  Follow-ups are a perfect opportunity to gather valuable feedback. Ask your clients how they're finding the product or service, and be open to hearing both the good and the bad. Constructive criticism is a goldmine for improvement and innovation. When you take their suggestions seriously and use them to make meaningful changes, you're showing that you value their input. For example, if a client suggests a minor tweak that improves the user experience, implementing that change can elevate your product while strengthening their trust in you. Feedback is not something

to shy away from; it's your roadmap to delivering even better service.

- **Building Rapport Through Continuous Engagement**:
  Don't let the relationship fizzle after the sale. Continuous engagement is key to keeping the connection alive. Small gestures like sending a thank-you note or offering a personalized discount can go a long way in showing your appreciation. You might also consider creating loyalty programs or offering exclusive rewards for repeat clients. When clients feel valued beyond their initial purchase, they're more likely to become loyal advocates for your brand. These small, thoughtful actions reinforce the idea that you're committed to their long-term satisfaction, not just a one-time transaction.

- **Demonstrating Appreciation**:
  Appreciation is often underrated but incredibly impactful. A simple thank-you note, a personalized gift, or even a public acknowledgment on social media can show your clients how much you value their business. People want to feel recognized and appreciated, and when you go out of your way to show gratitude, it strengthens the relationship. For example, a small token of appreciation—a branded gift or a handwritten note—can make your client feel seen and valued, increasing the likelihood of repeat business and positive word-of-mouth. These gestures might seem small, but they build a reservoir of goodwill that can serve your business for years to come.

Creating value beyond the sale isn't just about maintaining the client relationship—it's about continuously reinforcing the trust that brought them to you in the first place. Your clients should always feel that they made the right choice by working with you, not just at the time of the sale but throughout their journey with your product or service.

Chapter Takeaways

Building long-term relationships is the secret to thriving in sales. Sales is more than closing a single deal, instead, the focus should be on staying engaged with your clients over time and continuing to offer value. Trust is built and solidified through consistent, meaningful follow-ups, personalization, and ongoing efforts to ensure your clients' success. Your efforts to check in, listen, and resolve issues can transform a one-time buyer into a lifelong client who will not only come back to you but also refer you to others. By nurturing your client relationships, you're investing in a future of sustained success.

Here are some prompts to help you reflect and apply these lessons:

- Review your most recent client interactions. Are you consistently following up after meetings or sales? How can you improve the timing and frequency of your follow-ups to keep clients engaged?

- Consider how you can personalize your follow-ups. What specific details from your last conversation can you reference in your next message? How will this deepen your connection with your client?

- Reflect on a time when you didn't follow up, and think about the potential missed opportunity. How could staying engaged have helped build a stronger relationship?

- Create a post-sale follow-up plan. How often will you check in with your clients after the initial sale? What methods will you use to stay connected and add value after the deal is done?

- Think about how you can gather and use feedback to improve your offerings. How will you ask for feedback in a way that encourages honest, constructive responses? How will you use this information to enhance your products or services?

As you continue building lasting relationships, keep in mind that the foundation of every connection is understanding and trust. In our next conversation, we'll explore the often overlooked but critical role of emotional intelligence in sales. How can your ability to manage emotions—both yours and your client's—be the key to unlocking even deeper connections? There's more to come, and you'll want to dive deeper into the art of emotional connection.

Chapter 8: The Role of Emotional Intelligence in Sales

"The most important single ingredient in the formula of success is knowing how to get along with people." — Theodore Roosevelt.

Emotional intelligence (EQ) in sales goes beyond knowing your product or crafting the perfect pitch. You will find that it's about genuinely understanding people, their emotions, and how to build meaningful connections. Have you ever been in a conversation where the words being said or the tone of voice didn't match the energy in the room? You can feel it, right? That's emotional intelligence at play, and in sales, it's the key to building trust and rapport with your clients.

Think of EQ as the bridge between you and your client—it's what turns a sales interaction into a relationship. When you can read your client's emotions, respond with empathy, and manage your own reactions effectively, you create a space where your client feels truly understood. And let's face it, people want to buy from someone who "gets them," not just someone who's pushing a product.

I feel like the times I've thrived in sales had less to do with how well I knew the product and more to do with how well I connected emotionally. I remember once working with a client who was upset—really upset. Instead of getting defensive or rushing to explain, I paused. I took a breath, listened deeply, and realized their frustration wasn't about the product at all. It was about a lack of communication. By shifting the focus from defending the sale to understanding their concerns, I not only salvaged the situation, but I built trust that turned into a long-term relationship.

Enhancing Emotional Intelligence to Build Stronger Connections

Developing your emotional intelligence is a journey that evolves over time, impacting every relationship you build, whether it's with a client, a colleague, or someone in your personal life. Emotional intelligence is the key to deepening trust, fostering better communication, and understanding others in a way that goes beyond the surface level. It's tuning into the emotions and needs of those around you and using that awareness to create meaningful, lasting relationships.

Think back to the strongest connections you've made in your life. Were they built purely on facts and logic? Probably not. The best relationships, the ones that stand the test of time, are grounded in emotional understanding and empathy. Whether it's a trusted friend, a close family member, or even a loyal client, emotional intelligence plays a central role in creating that bond. It's the unspoken language that says, "I get you," and that simple but powerful acknowledgment makes all the difference.

When you apply this concept to sales, the results can be transformative. As salespeople, sometimes we naturally get caught up in our own desires such as closing deals and meeting quotas. We must stay rooted in the human connection that affects the client if we want to maximize our success. Clients are looking to buy a product, but by genuinely understanding their needs, challenges, and concerns, you add an extra level of comfort and attraction as a salesperson. They want to feel heard and valued. And when you demonstrate emotional intelligence—by truly listening, empathizing, and responding thoughtfully—you show that you're there for more than just a transaction. You're there to help, and that's when trust begins to take root.

I've found that the more you invest in developing your emotional intelligence, the more it enriches your interactions—not just in sales, but in every part of your life. You'll notice that you're able to handle stress more effectively, communicate more clearly, and create stronger connections with those around you. You might even find that difficult conversations become easier because you're able to navigate emotions—both yours and others—with greater ease.

And here's the beauty of it: Emotional intelligence is something you can continuously improve. It's not a destination but an ongoing process of self-awareness, empathy, and growth. With every interaction, you have the chance to learn more about yourself and those you engage with. As you develop this skill, your relationships—both personal and professional—will reflect the effort you put into understanding and connecting with people on a deeper level.

The more you nurture your emotional intelligence, the more rewarding your journey becomes. To be a better salesperson, focusing on becoming a better communicator, a more empathetic leader, and a more compassionate human being should be your key focuses in the realm of EQ. And when you bring that kind of energy into your relationships, the impact is undeniable.

The question is: How much could your sales career—and your life—transform if you fully embraced the power of emotional intelligence?

Managing Your Own Emotions and Reactions

Along with keeping a cool head when things get tough, managing your own emotions is mastering the art of responding thoughtfully rather than reacting impulsively. This is a point of adversity for many. There's a big difference between understanding your emotions and controlling them effectively. Emotional intelligence requires you to know when to pause, reflect, and choose the most constructive response. How many times have you let frustration or anger seep into a conversation, only to regret it later? In sales, where the stakes can often feel high, your ability to manage emotions—especially in challenging situations—can make the difference between salvaging a deal and losing a client.

When you're interacting with clients, you may think that your words are the only thing that you're communicating through; but they are also feeling your energy. If you come across as defensive or frustrated, that energy sets the tone for the conversation. On the other hand, maintaining calm and demonstrating control sends a powerful message. You're not someone selling a product; you're a person clients can rely on—someone who doesn't crumble under pressure. And that, in itself, is a hallmark of emotional maturity and professionalism.

- **Self-Reflection**: One of the best tools for emotional management is self-reflection. After every significant interaction, especially the tough ones, take a moment to ask yourself: "How did I handle that? Did I let my emotions get the best of me, or did I stay in control?" Journaling can be incredibly insightful here. Writing down how you reacted and how you felt during a stressful situation helps you identify patterns. Are there certain triggers that consistently push your buttons? Do you notice that you react differently when you're tired or under pressure? Once you start recognizing these patterns, you can take steps to manage them better the next time around.

For example, when I feel rushed or under pressure, I'm more likely to react quickly and emotionally, which often doesn't end well. But when I take time to reflect on these moments, I realize there's always a better way I could have handled them. Reflection doesn't just help you become more aware of your emotions; it gives you the tools to respond more thoughtfully in the future.

- **Self-Regulation**: This is where the real power of emotional intelligence comes in. It's easy to let emotions take the driver's seat, but self-regulation is about pausing before you hit the gas. Let's say you're dealing with an unhappy client. They're frustrated, maybe even a little confrontational. Your initial reaction might be to defend yourself, explain why it's not your fault, or push back. But what if you paused? What if, instead of reacting defensively, you took a deep breath, allowed their emotions to settle, and then responded calmly?

I can tell you from experience that the simple act of pausing can transform an entire conversation. Giving yourself that moment to breathe and think creates space for a more logical and composed response. And when clients see that you're not reacting emotionally, they're more likely to calm down as well. It's almost like you're setting the emotional tone of the conversation, and your calmness can be contagious.

- **Conflict Resolution**: Let's be real—conflict is inevitable. But how you handle it can either strengthen or weaken a relationship. When things go wrong—and they will—it's easy to fall into the trap of blame. But that's not what clients need. What they need is a solution. If an order is delayed or a product isn't what they expected, your first instinct should be to resolve the issue, not explain why it happened.

I've seen it happen time and time again: salespeople waste valuable time trying to justify or explain a mistake, while the client just wants to know how it will be fixed. Shift your focus from explaining the problem to offering a solution. For instance, if a product has a malfunction and didn't work when the client received it, instead of diving into logistics and what went wrong, ask, "How can I make this right for you?" It's a simple shift, but it immediately changes the dynamic of the conversation. You're no longer on the defensive; you're offering support. This not only resolves the conflict faster but also reassures the client that you're on their side, working toward a solution.

Managing emotions in sales isn't always about staying calm under pressure; but using every situation—good or bad—as an opportunity to build trust. Most clients desire perfection which, is the goal, but more reasonably they expect professionalism. When you consistently show that you can handle difficult situations with grace and focus on resolving problems rather than escalating them, you'll earn their respect and loyalty.

Reading and Responding to Customer Emotions Effectively

There are two parts to emotional intelligence. The first part is the focus of managing your own emotions, in which we just covered. This makes up the beef of EQ because it's the part we can really control. The second part, as you might have figured out, is reading and adjusting to your client emotions. Not every client will come out and tell you how they're feeling. Sometimes, you need to pick up on non-verbal cues or read between the lines.

When a client is quiet or hesitant, it's essential to pay attention to their body language. Some individuals naturally feel uncomfortable making eye contact, and this is simply their way of interacting. To tell the difference, pay close attention to their behavior and focus on their train of thought. Observe whether they seem preoccupied or distracted, or if they're deliberately avoiding eye contact. Understanding their state of mind is key, and sometimes, that's all you can really do. Do they seem tense or distracted? These subtle signs can give you insight into what they're feeling, even if they're not saying it outright. By understanding these cues, you can adjust your approach and respond in a way that acknowledges their emotions. For instance, if a client seems unsure, you might say, "I sense that something is holding you back. Let's talk about it."

Body language offers valuable insight into a customer's emotions, often conveying what words do not. Notice their facial expressions; a genuine smile can indicate openness or satisfaction, while a frown or furrowed brow might reveal confusion or frustration. Hand movements are also telling—crossed arms or restless hands could suggest defensiveness or impatience, whereas open gestures and a relaxed posture typically signal a more comfortable and receptive state. Pay attention to how a client positions themselves; if they face you directly and appear relaxed, it shows they are engaged and at ease in the conversation. Conversely, if they shift their weight or angle their body away, it may indicate discomfort, hesitation, or impatience.

Responding with empathy is absolutely essential. When clients feel genuinely heard and understood, they are much more likely to trust you. Validating their emotions—whether they're feeling frustrated, excited, or uncertain—demonstrates that you're truly in sync with them. Give them the space they need to express their thoughts and feelings without interruption; sometimes, the most powerful way to build trust is simply by being a patient, attentive listener.

It's also crucial not to push clients, especially those who aren't immediately open. The goal is to make them as comfortable as possible, taking any pressure off. When clients feel pressured or uncomfortable—regardless of who is responsible for it—they're likely to pull back in order to protect their emotional security. Ensuring that they feel safe and unpressured is key to maintaining trust.

Adjusting your approach based on a client's body language and emotional cues is a fundamental aspect of effective communication. For instance, if a client appears tense, with crossed arms or limited eye contact, it's important to create a more relaxed environment. You can do this by softening your tone, offering reassurance, and asking open-ended questions that invite them to share more comfortably. Conversely, if the client seems engaged, with open and confident body language, you can match their energy by being more direct and enthusiastic in your responses. By mirroring their emotional state, you show empathy and establish a stronger connection, making them feel understood and more likely to trust your guidance.

Chapter Takeaways

Emotional intelligence is one of the most powerful tools in sales. It's all about understanding yourself and others on a deeper level, managing your emotions effectively, and responding to clients in ways that build trust and strengthen relationships. Whether through self-reflection, practicing empathy, or mastering the art of conflict resolution, your ability to connect emotionally with your clients is what will set you apart.

But don't forget—emotional intelligence is a lifelong journey. Every interaction is an opportunity to grow, learn, and improve. As you continue honing these skills, you'll not only become a better salesperson but also a better communicator, leader, and friend. Now, let's take some time to reflect on how you can apply emotional intelligence in your sales interactions:

Here are a few exercises to help guide you:

- **Reflect on a recent client interaction:** Did you manage your emotions effectively, or did you allow frustration or stress to take over? What would you do differently next time to ensure a more composed and thoughtful response?

- **Practice self-regulation:** Throughout this week, whenever you feel your emotions rising, take a moment to pause before reacting. Observe how this changes the dynamic of your conversations and whether it leads to more positive outcomes.

- **Focus on empathy:** Make a conscious effort to validate your clients' emotions in your next few interactions. Notice how this affects the rapport and trust between you and the client.

- **Develop your self-reflection routine:** Set aside time at the end of each day to journal about your emotional responses in sales situations. Identify patterns and areas for improvement.

- **Hone your non-verbal communication skills:** Pay close attention to your clients' body language in upcoming meetings. What cues can you pick up, and how can you adjust your approach based on their non-verbal signals?

And as we wrap up this discussion on emotional intelligence, think about how these skills can help you manage your clients and overcome obstacles in your sales journey. In our next conversation, we'll delve into how to face and overcome challenges while sustaining the trust you've worked so hard to build. Trust is fragile, but with the right tools, you can ensure it remains strong despite difficulties.

Your Insights Can Make a Difference!

I want to speak from the heart and ask for a moment of your time. If this book has resonated with you, sparked new ideas, or even just provided a fresh perspective, I'd be incredibly grateful if you could leave a **positive review** on Amazon. Your feedback is way for others to see the value you've found, a guide for those on the fence about whether this book is worth their time. Your review could be the nudge someone else needs to make a decision that could shape their business or career.

Think of it this way: just as trust is built one interaction at a time, reviews are the stepping stones that build credibility for this book. Every word you share helps strengthen the trust others will place in it. And to me, your feedback means the world. It's what keeps this journey going, helping refine future content and ensuring that each chapter continues to bring real value to readers like you. Your voice matters, and I'd be honored if you shared it.

Chapter 9: Navigating Trust-Breaking Situations

"It takes years to build a reputation and minutes to ruin it." — Will Rogers.

Building trust is the foundation of any long-term relationship in sales, but what happens when that trust is broken? The harsh reality is that trust, once damaged, can be difficult to restore, yet it's not impossible. We've all experienced situations where a client felt let down—whether it was due to a mistake, miscommunication, or external factors beyond our control. When trust falters, it's essential to recognize that what matters most is how you respond.

The Impact of Broken Trust

Broken trust doesn't always stem from a monumental mistake. In fact, it's often the accumulation of smaller, seemingly insignificant issues that can have the most damaging effects. Imagine you're working with a client and you miss a deadline—not by much, but enough to inconvenience them. Then, a week later, you forget to follow up on an email. Again, it seems minor. These little oversights may not feel like major failures, but they start to add up. Over time, they plant seeds of doubt in your client's mind. It's not a single event that breaks trust; the slow erosion of confidence leaves the biggest mark.

I recall an experience early in my career where I missed a small but significant detail in a project. To me, it seemed like a minor hiccup, something I could quickly rectify. But to my client, it was a sign of carelessness, and it made them second-guess my reliability.

Even though the overall project went smoothly, that one detail lingered, creating a small crack in the foundation of our relationship. From that moment on, I realized trust is more than about doing things right but also handling things well when they go wrong.

Let me share a story that illustrates this. Picture two salespeople, both skilled in their field—let's call them Sarah and Michael. Sarah has always been attentive to her clients, ensuring every detail is addressed. One day, she misses a small deadline, just by a few hours. Instead of ignoring it or hoping the client wouldn't notice, she immediately acknowledges the mistake, apologizes sincerely, and takes responsibility. She even goes the extra mile by offering a small incentive to make up for the inconvenience. Her client, while initially disappointed, quickly forgives her because she was honest, proactive, and showed that she cared about their experience.

Now, let's look at Michael. He's equally skilled but tends to overlook minor details, assuming his clients won't be bothered by them. One day, he also misses a deadline. Instead of addressing it, he lets it slide, thinking it's not a big deal. His client notices but says nothing. A week later, Michael forgets to send a follow-up email. The client begins to wonder if he's really as reliable as they initially thought. Although Michael doesn't see it, the client is slowly losing trust. A few weeks later, the client decides to take their business elsewhere, even though nothing catastrophic occurred. It wasn't about the big things—it was the small, repeated actions that chipped away at the client's confidence.

These two examples highlight how broken trust can unfold in subtle ways. In Sarah's case, she recognized the trust-breaking moment right away and took action to fix it. She didn't wait for the client to bring it up; she owned the mistake, which strengthened her client's trust in her. On the other hand, Michael didn't recognize the issue until it was too late. His lack of awareness and follow-through led to the gradual erosion of trust.

Recognizing trust-breaking events can be tricky because they don't always come with a neon sign. Clients may not always tell you when something is wrong. Sometimes, they'll just distance themselves quietly. This is why staying attuned to the subtle cues in your communication is so important. Has the client's tone changed? Are they responding less frequently or with shorter, more curt replies? These could be signs that something has gone awry. And if you ignore those signs, you risk letting the issue grow.

I've learned that the longer you wait to repair broken trust, the harder it becomes. Trust is fragile—once a client begins to question your reliability or integrity, they'll start looking for alternatives. They may not tell you outright that they've lost faith, but they'll start exploring other options. Acting quickly to repair the situation shows that you're committed to the relationship and willing to take responsibility for your actions.

Here's a key lesson: Trust isn't about being perfect. It's about being accountable. Clients don't expect you to never make mistakes—they expect you to own up to them and fix them. In fact, clients are often more impressed by how you handle mistakes than by the mistake itself. They appreciate your effort to make things right, whether the original issue was your fault or not. The sincerity and urgency in your response will determine whether the trust is repaired or broken for good.

In both Sarah's and Michael's cases, a mistake was made, but their approaches to handling it made all the difference. Sarah's client trusted her more after she addressed the issue, while Michael's client quietly walked away. The difference? Proactive accountability.

Trust, once broken, can be difficult to rebuild, but it's not impossible. The key is to recognize the issue early, take responsibility, and put in the effort to make things right. As I've learned from my own experiences, it's often not the mistake itself that matters most but how you respond that leaves the lasting impression.

Identifying and Addressing Trust Issues

Trust can be fragile, and when it's shaken, it's not always obvious. Recognizing when trust has been damaged is often the most challenging part. Clients rarely come forward and say, "I don't trust you anymore." Instead, the signs are subtle and often masked by politeness or a desire to avoid confrontation. So how do you know when trust has been compromised? It's the little things: a shift in tone, a client who suddenly becomes less responsive, or even someone who was once very engaged becoming increasingly passive in communication. These subtle shifts are the first red flags, and as a professional, you need to be keenly aware of them. Trust me, it's far easier to address these early signs than to wait until the relationship is on the verge of collapse. So how do you spot these red flags and turn the situation around before it's too late?

- **Detecting the Problem:** Identifying trust issues isn't as straightforward as someone flat-out telling you they're unhappy. Clients, especially in professional settings, often hesitate to vocalize their concerns directly. They might fear confrontation or feel uncomfortable admitting their doubts. Instead, they often express their discomfort in more subtle ways. Perhaps a client who once eagerly participated in discussions is now giving one-word answers, or their once-friendly tone has become formal and distant. Maybe they're asking a lot more clarifying questions, signaling that they no longer have full confidence in your recommendations. These are your cues.

I've seen cases where clients suddenly start looping in other team members to conversations that used to be one-on-one. That's a quiet sign that they might be losing trust in your ability to manage things independently. Pay attention to these signs. The sooner you detect the issue, the quicker you can address it before it spirals into something bigger. It's not always comfortable to ask, "Is everything okay?" but it's far better than letting the problem fester. It's crucial to develop your emotional intelligence (EQ) because it helps you recognize the subtle signs of broken trust that clients may express. These cues can be hard to spot, but with a well-developed EQ, you'll be more attuned to the small hints and signals that indicate a client's trust might be wavering.

- **The Power of Follow-Up:** One of the most effective ways to address potential trust issues is through proactive follow-up. Follow-ups reinforce the commitment you've already shown by keeping everything on track and ensuring no detail is overlooked. It's a proactive way to demonstrate that your client's experience remains a priority, addressing any potential trust concerns before they even arise. Follow-ups can serve as a lifeline in relationships that may be teetering on the edge of a trust breakdown. Imagine this: You've completed a project for a client, but something feels off. Maybe they've gone quiet, or their enthusiasm has waned. Instead of waiting for them to come to you, take the initiative to reach out. A simple, well-crafted follow-up message can go a long way. For instance:

"Hi [Client's Name],
I hope this message finds you well. I wanted to check in on

the [project/delivery] and see how everything is going from your side. Please let me know if there's anything you need or if there's anything I can do to ensure things are running smoothly. Your satisfaction is my top priority, and I'm here to help with any concerns or adjustments. Looking forward to hearing from you."

This kind of message opens the door for the client to express any concerns they might have, giving you the chance to address them before they escalate. It shows that you're paying attention and genuinely care about their experience, which is key to rebuilding or maintaining trust. To take this example over the top, use your personalization skills to make your client really feel special

- **Transparency and Apology:** Mistakes are never enjoyable, but the fact is, everyone makes them. The difference between a professional who earns trust and one who loses it is how they handle those mistakes. When you've made an error—whether it's a miscommunication, a missed deadline, or something more significant—how you respond is crucial. The first thing you need to do is own up to the mistake. Transparency is non-negotiable. Clients can sense when you're skirting around the issue or downplaying it. The best course of action is to be upfront and offer a sincere apology, without trying to sugarcoat or make excuses. For example:

"Hi [Client's Name],
I wanted to take a moment to address an oversight on my end. I realize that [specific issue] didn't go as planned, and I take full responsibility for it. I'm committed to making this right, and I'll ensure this doesn't happen again. Please know that your satisfaction is extremely important to me,

and I'm here to correct this in any way that would best serve you."

Notice that this apology doesn't dilute responsibility with excuses. It's direct and takes ownership of the issue. This kind of sincerity goes a long way in regaining a client's trust. Remember, clients appreciate honesty. They don't expect you to be perfect, but they do expect you to be accountable.

Remember, the client isn't interested in who's responsible for the mistake. That detail doesn't matter to them, even if it feels like their frustration is directed at you personally. To them, you're simply the representative of the issue. In reality, what they care about most is having the problem resolved so they can move forward.

- **Personalized Compensation:** In some cases, an apology isn't enough to fully restore trust, and that's where offering personalized compensation can make a real difference. Depending on the nature of the issue, you might consider offering a discount, a free upgrade, or even a full refund. But here's the key: the compensation needs to feel thoughtful and specific to the client's situation. A generic offer can come across as a half-hearted attempt to fix the problem.

Let's say you're a web designer who missed a critical deadline, and the client's product launch was delayed. Simply apologizing might not be enough. In this case, offering something like:

"To make up for the delay, I'd like to offer you a complimentary site optimization package as a gesture of

goodwill. I want to ensure you're getting the best possible experience from our collaboration."

This kind of offer shows you've thought about how the delay affected the client and are providing something valuable in return. It's not just about offering compensation—it's about demonstrating that you care enough to tailor the solution to their needs. Personalized compensation makes the client feel valued, and it reinforces that you're willing to go above and beyond to make things right.

Rebuilding broken trust is ultimately about proving, through your actions, that you're dedicated to earning it back. Whether through a heartfelt apology, meaningful compensation, or steady follow-up, the aim is to show that the relationship matters to you and that you're committed to restoring their confidence.

Learning from Trust-Related Failures

Mistakes are inevitable in any business relationship, but they don't have to signal the end of trust. Instead, they can serve as opportunities to strengthen your relationships if approached correctly. When a mistake happens, it's essential to view it not as a failure, but as a moment of growth. Take a step back and reflect: Was the problem due to miscommunication, a missed deadline, or perhaps unclear expectations? Whatever the cause, addressing the root of the issue not only resolves the immediate problem but also prevents it from recurring. It's a bit like breaking a bone. When a bone breaks, it's undoubtedly painful and can be a serious issue. However, the remarkable thing is that your body can heal the bone, not just restoring it to its original state but actually making it even stronger in the process. Every mistake can become a valuable lesson, refining how you handle future interactions and helping you build a more resilient approach to maintaining trust.

As you might know, trust can be damaged from more than missed deadlines and poor communication. Sometimes, trust falters when expectations aren't managed properly. Over-promising and under-delivering is a common issue. Think about how many times you've heard someone say, "I'll get this to you by the end of the day," only for the deadline to pass without any updates. Clients rely on your word, and when those promises aren't fulfilled, trust erodes. Managing expectations means being honest about what can be delivered and when, ensuring that clients are never left wondering about the status of a project.

Another area where trust can break down is a lack of transparency. Clients want to feel informed every step of the way. If they feel kept in the dark or receive limited updates, doubt creeps in. Have you ever found yourself waiting for a response, unsure if the other person is even working on your request? That uncertainty can be damaging. Keeping clients in the loop—whether the news is good or bad—helps maintain the sense that they are valued and their concerns matter.

Attention to detail is another key area where trust can tremble. Missing small but important details—whether in emails, contracts, or even in conversations—signals to the client that you may not be fully engaged. These small slip-ups can build up over time, leading to larger trust issues. Clients want to feel like they are your priority, and when mistakes happen, it can shake their confidence in your reliability. Simply fact-check everything the best you can. This is also an opportunity to demonstrate transparency. If you're unsure about any detail, be straightforward and ask for clarification. Not only does this show that you care about getting things right, but it can also provide relief to the client, assuring them that you prioritize accuracy and their satisfaction above all.

It shows that you're committed to doing things correctly, reinforcing the trust you've built.

Then there's accountability. It's easy to get defensive or make excuses when something goes wrong. But clients appreciate transparency and ownership. Instead of dodging responsibility, face the issue head-on. An apology doesn't need to be an admission of incompetence; it's a way to show clients their trust matters to you. By owning your mistakes, you demonstrate integrity, which can do more to repair the relationship than trying to deflect blame.

Once the issue has been addressed, the next critical step is letting your clients know what you've done to fix it. It's not enough to quietly resolve the problem behind the scenes. Clients need to see that you've taken proactive steps to ensure the mistake won't happen again. By communicating your actions to prevent future issues, you reassure them that their concerns have been taken seriously. This also shows that you're not just focused on solving the immediate issue but are committed to improving the long-term relationship.

If a mistake impacts multiple clients or even your broader reputation, it's crucial to address the issue both publicly and personally. For instance, if you're a salesperson and a processing error leads to several clients receiving the wrong product, start by sending a general email to all affected clients. In this message, acknowledge the error, explain what happened, and outline the steps you're taking to resolve it. However, don't stop there—follow up with personal phone calls to each client. Apologize sincerely, listen to their concerns, and offer specific solutions tailored to their situation, such as expediting a replacement or providing a discount on future orders. If a client needed the product urgently for an event, offer to overnight the replacement. Taking the time to address each client individually shows that you value their business and are committed to making things right. By being transparent, accepting responsibility, and offering personalized resolutions, you can transform a potentially damaging situation into an opportunity to strengthen trust and build stronger relationships.

Navigating trust-related failures is about turning a difficult situation into an opportunity for growth. When handled with transparency, accountability, and clear communication, a mistake doesn't have to mean the end of the relationship. Instead, it can strengthen the bond, reinforcing the idea that trust, once rebuilt, can be even stronger than before.

Chapter Takeaways

Broken trust can happen in an instant, but repairing it requires thoughtful, consistent effort. The key takeaway here is that trust isn't just built through perfection but through accountability. You will make mistakes. What matters is how you respond to them. Whether it's following up, apologizing, or offering compensation, every step you take to rebuild trust strengthens your relationship with the client. When you actively address the issues and show your commitment, you not only repair the damage but often leave the relationship stronger than before.

Exercises and Prompts for Reflection:

1. **Reflect on a time when you made a mistake with a client.** How did you address it? What steps did you take to rebuild trust, and what could you have done differently?

2. **Evaluate your follow-up strategy.** Are you proactively checking in with clients to ensure they are satisfied, or are you waiting for problems to arise? How can you improve this process?

3. **Think about your approach to apologizing.** Have you ever diluted an apology with excuses? How can you offer a more sincere and transparent apology in future situations?

4. **Consider a recent issue with a client.** What personalized compensation could you offer to show your commitment to resolving the problem? How can you tailor your response to meet the specific needs of that client?

5. **Identify a potential trust issue in your current client relationships.** What steps can you take to address it before it escalates into a larger problem?

Trust is not just about the immediate interactions you have with clients; it is about how those interactions compound over time. Our next conversation will explore what it means to scale trust in larger teams and how you can build a culture of reliability that extends beyond individual relationships to your entire organization.

Chapter 10: The Role of Social Media in Building Trust

"Authenticity, honesty, and personal voice underlie much of what's successful on social media." — Rick Levine.

Your presence on social media is often the first impression potential clients will have of you or your business. Think about how many times you've checked someone's profile or scanned through their posts before deciding whether to engage with them. In the sales world, that initial glance at your profile can either build trust or create doubt. This is why optimizing your social media profiles is so crucial. Every detail, from your bio to your profile picture, should reflect who you are and what your brand stands for. A complete, professional, and authentic profile sets the stage for trust. People want to know that they're engaging with someone credible, and this is your first opportunity to show them that you're reliable, approachable, and aligned with their needs.

But having a great profile is just the beginning. Imagine visiting a professional page, perhaps one of a competitor, only to find that the last post was six months ago. How would that make you feel? Chances are, you'd question their relevance, reliability, or even if they're still in business. That's the power of consistency—or the lack of it. To truly build trust, you need to be consistent in how you show up. Posting regular, valuable content doesn't just keep you in your audience's mind—it establishes you as a knowledgeable and reliable source in your industry. It's like meeting a friend who always shares useful insights when you see them. You come to value and trust their input, right? Similarly, when you share industry insights, tips, or success stories, you're showing that you know what you're talking about and that you're committed to helping others grow.

Whether you're posting a detailed breakdown of industry trends or a simple success story from one of your clients, your content sends a powerful message: you're not just here for yourself; you're here to provide value. And that's something people can trust.

Consistency also sets the stage for thought leadership. Social media platforms like LinkedIn and X are invaluable tools for building credibility—an essential component of the Trust Equation. Think of them as a stage where you can not only showcase your expertise but also demonstrate the consistency that underpins trustworthiness. It's not enough to simply show up; you must engage meaningfully and consistently over time to get the best results.

By publishing articles, joining industry discussions, or participating in conversations on relevant topics, you're showing that you're actively involved in your field. This consistent presence positions you as an authority, someone whose insights are valued. When people repeatedly see your name associated with insightful discussions and valuable posts, they begin to see you as a credible source—one they can rely on for trustworthy advice and ideas. You become a "go-to" figure, and that credibility fosters a natural trust in your voice and perspective.

After all, people are drawn to those who consistently provide them with value and insight rather than those who only appear occasionally with attention-grabbing headlines. Building that kind of credibility isn't a one-time effort; it's an ongoing process that lays the foundation for lasting trust.

And while you're building that credibility, another powerful tool comes into play: collaboration. Engaging with influencers or well-respected voices in your industry adds another layer to your trust-building efforts. Think about it—if you see someone you already trust engaging with or endorsing a new voice, aren't you more likely to trust them too? This is the magic of social proof. When you align yourself with individuals who have already gained credibility, you borrow some of that credibility for yourself. It's not about chasing after celebrity endorsements, but more about fostering relationships with those who have earned respect in your niche. You don't need a big name to build trust, but having the endorsement or even just the visible engagement of a respected figure in your field can be a game-changer.

This collaboration is such a powerful tool that it's used at the highest levels. For example, major athleticwear brands partner with famous athletes to influence consumers and persuade them to buy their products. Similarly, prominent political figures often seek endorsements from celebrities or other well-known public figures to gain the support and interest of voters and various groups. The influence and reach these individuals have can sway a large number of people toward—or against—a particular mission or cause. It's a strategic alignment that amplifies credibility and trust.

These relationships, however, aren't about seeking favors. They are built through consistent, meaningful interactions—engaging in real, thoughtful conversations that demonstrate genuine value and alignment of interests.

Still, none of this works if you're not responsive. Imagine going into a shop, asking for help, and being completely ignored. Would you trust that business? Probably not. The same thing happens on social media when comments, questions, or direct messages go unanswered. Being attentive and responsive signals that you care about your audience. It's not enough to just post content and walk away—social media is a two-way street. By engaging with your audience, responding to their inquiries promptly, and acknowledging their contributions, you're showing that you value them. This is where relationships deepen. When someone comments on your post or sends you a message, it's an invitation to build trust. Responding quickly and thoughtfully lays the groundwork for ongoing dialogue, demonstrating that you're not just there to promote yourself—but to build a community. And when people feel heard, they're much more likely to trust you.

So, how are you currently showing up on social media? Are you being consistent? Are you engaging with thought leaders or just passively scrolling? And most importantly, are you actively engaging with your audience, or are you merely broadcasting? Trust doesn't come from a one-sided conversation; it's built in the back-and-forth of authentic engagement.

Engaging with Authenticity

The heart of building trust on social media lies in authenticity. It's tempting to automate responses or stick to canned messages, but people can tell when you're being robotic. Genuine conversations make all the difference. Tailoring your responses and interacting with your audience meaningfully shows that you truly care about their thoughts, concerns, and experiences. For instance, think about the last time someone took a genuine interest in something you said online. Didn't it make you feel heard and valued? That's the kind of connection people crave, which turns casual followers into loyal advocates.

Let's be real—when you scroll through social media, it's easy to spot the difference between someone who's genuinely engaged and someone who's just going through the motions. Imagine reaching out to a brand with a question, and instead of getting a personal response, you receive a generic, automated message that doesn't address your query. How does that make you feel? It's disappointing, right? Now compare that to a time when you received a thoughtful, personalized reply that directly addressed your concern. That's the difference authenticity makes. It's about making your audience feel seen and understood, not just another number in your follower count.

Authenticity also means transparency. Be upfront about your strengths, but don't shy away from admitting your limitations. If a product or service isn't right for a customer, don't force it—recommend an alternative. Think about how refreshing it is to deal with someone who is willing to say, "This might not be the best fit for you, but here's something that could work better." Clients appreciate this kind of honesty because it shows that you're not just focused on making a sale; you're genuinely looking out for their best interests. It's easy to spot when someone's pushing a product just to meet a quota, but when you put the client first, that level of integrity resonates. Trust me, people remember it, and they're far more likely to come back to you in the future because they know they can rely on your honest judgment.

Recently, I was chatting with a friend about a tough choice he was facing with his son's baseball team. He had two options: stick with the team his son had been on for years, where he knew the coach was honest, genuine, and always put the players' best interests first, or join a new team with most of his son's future middle school teammates. Joining the new team would help his son start building connections that would carry over into middle school, a clear advantage. But leaving behind a trusted coach wasn't easy, so he decided to talk it over with him.

When he spoke with the coach, the response wasn't what you'd expect. The coach said, "I'd love to keep your son on the team, and we'd benefit from having him, but it would be best for him to start playing with his future teammates." My friend shared how difficult it was to hear this—he knew the coach was right, but that same honesty was what made leaving the team so hard. The lesson here?

When you're genuine and act with integrity, even if it means encouraging others to choose a path that might not benefit you, people recognize and appreciate it. They remember it, and it deepens their respect and trust in you.

Another key to authenticity is humanizing your brand. People trust people, not faceless companies. So how can you add that personal touch? Share behind-the-scenes content—let your audience see the faces behind the brand. Introduce your team, show how you work, highlight your company values, or even share a personal story. Think about how much more connected you feel to a brand when you know the people behind it. For example, a simple team photo or a video showing the process of creating a product can make your brand feel more relatable. When your audience sees the human side of your work, they're more likely to connect with you on a personal level. And once that connection is made, trust naturally follows. It's the same reason why an upwards of 70% of people say they'd rather buy from a local shop where they know the owner by name than from a giant corporation with no face.

But authenticity is making more out of showing up, such as creating a dialogue. Social media shouldn't be a one-sided conversation where you're just broadcasting your message to the masses. Instead, it should feel like an ongoing conversation where both sides actively participate. Ask for your audience's opinions, respond to their feedback, and engage in meaningful discussions. If someone takes the time to leave a comment on your post, make sure you respond thoughtfully. Don't just hit "like" and move on. Think about it: when was the last time you felt valued by a brand that took the time to really engage with you? When people feel like they're part of the conversation, rather than just being talked at, they're more likely to trust the person on the other side of the screen. They want to know that their voice matters and that you're not just pushing your agenda.

As we discussed before, it is important to address mistakes right away and out in the open. Everyone makes them, and your audience knows this. Trying to appear perfect or brushing mistakes under the rug can often do more harm than good. Admitting mistakes publicly can be a powerful trust-building tool. It's a bold move, but one that can pay off massively. No one is perfect, and trying to maintain an image of perfection can often backfire. Acknowledging an error and openly discussing how you plan to fix it shows that you're accountable and committed to improving. For example, let's say your company made a product recall or had an issue with customer service. Instead of covering it up or making excuses, addressing it directly and explaining how you're making things right can actually deepen trust. Customers value transparency over perfection because it feels more human

Admitting mistakes is not a sign of weakness—it's a sign of authenticity and strength. It shows that you value honesty and transparency above all, and that's something people respect. A brand that can admit its flaws and show genuine effort to improve often earns more loyalty than one that pretends nothing ever goes wrong. After all, trust is built on the foundation of honesty. The more transparent and authentic you are, the stronger that trust becomes.

So, ask yourself: when was the last time you had a meaningful conversation with your audience? When did you show the human side of your brand? And how often do you prioritize transparency, even when it's uncomfortable? Authenticity isn't just about what you say—it's about how you show up, engage, and handle both the highs and the lows.

Handling Negative Feedback Publicly

Dealing with negative feedback is inevitable, but how you respond to it is what sets you apart. Think about the last time you had a frustrating experience with a product or service. How did the company respond? Did they take forever to get back to you, or did they address your concerns right away? The difference is striking, isn't it? Responding promptly to negative feedback shows that you care about your customers' experience and that their satisfaction is your priority. When someone voices dissatisfaction, a delayed response can feel like you're ignoring the issue. The quicker you address it, the more you demonstrate your commitment to resolving the problem. Imagine airing a grievance and hearing nothing back—it leaves a bad taste, doesn't it? A timely response not only softens the frustration but also opens the door to rebuilding trust.

But a fast response alone isn't enough. How you respond matters just as much. Negative feedback can feel personal, especially when it's critical of something you've worked hard on, but reacting emotionally or defensively will only make things worse. Ever seen a social media thread where a brand gets defensive, and the situation spirals out of control? It never ends well. Remaining calm and professional in your responses is crucial. Your audience isn't just the person leaving the feedback; it's everyone who sees how you handle it. By keeping your tone respectful and composed, you show that you're in control and focused on finding a solution, not getting into a heated back-and-forth. Staying calm gives you the upper hand and shows that you prioritize your client's concerns over your ego.

In 2017, United Airlines faced a significant public relations crisis that serves as a real-life example of how a defensive response can escalate a situation. After overbooking a flight, the airline requested volunteers to give up their seats. When not enough passengers came forward, they forcibly removed a passenger from the plane. The incident was captured on video and quickly went viral, drawing widespread criticism for the airline's apparent lack of empathy. The CEO's initial statement, referring to the removal as "re-accommodating" passengers, further fueled public outrage.

As the backlash grew, United's response was perceived as defensive and disconnected from the public's concerns. The company eventually had to issue several apologies, revise its policies, and implement new staff training programs. This incident illustrates how a lack of empathy and defensive communication can severely damage a brand's reputation.

A critical part of handling negative feedback is acknowledging the issue directly. People want to feel heard, and sometimes the mere act of saying, "I understand why you're upset, and I'm sorry this happened," can defuse a tense situation. Consider how many times have you just wanted your complaint to be validated? Customers can often except imperfection, in turn they expect empathy. Ignoring or dismissing their frustration only fuels their anger. By taking the time to acknowledge their experience, you show that you're human, and humans make mistakes. But humans also have the ability to listen, empathize, and make things right.

After acknowledging the issue, the next step is crucial: offer solutions, not excuses. Offering excuses shifts the blame, whether on circumstances, other people, or the customer themselves, and it worsens the situation. Think about how frustrated you feel when someone brushes off your complaint with an excuse—it feels dismissive, like they're not taking you seriously. On the other hand, offering a real solution shows that you take responsibility and are willing to correct the mistake. Whether it's a refund, replacement, or some other form of resolution, your goal should be to make the customer feel valued and respected. Solutions say, "I hear you, and I'm going to make this right." Excuses say, "It's not my fault, and you're overreacting." Which response would you rather receive?

But there's more to negative feedback than resolving the immediate issue. Every piece of criticism is an opportunity to improve. Instead of seeing it as an attack, why not view it as a chance to grow?

Let's revisit the broken bone example. It's not about being upset with the doctor for diagnosing the broken bone; it's normal to feel frustrated about the injury itself. But at least now you know what's wrong, and that knowledge allows you to seek a solution, whether it's surgery, a cast, or a splint. Similarly, once the bone heals, it often comes back stronger. In the same way, identifying and addressing issues will help improve the customer experience for future clients, making your business more resilient and trusted.

By treating negative feedback as a learning moment, you not only fix the issue for one customer but also improve the experience for future customers. How many companies do you know that use negative feedback to improve themselves? The brands that take criticism seriously and evolve because of it are the ones that build long-term trust with their audience. When you communicate the steps you're taking to address the feedback, you show that you're committed to continuous improvement, not just damage control. This strengthens your relationship with the individual who had the issue and signals to your wider audience that you care about getting better.

Let's not forget that turning a negative into a positive can do wonders for your brand. Customers who see you've genuinely addressed their concerns often become your biggest advocates. They'll tell others about how well you handled their issue, and word-of-mouth trust is one of the most powerful marketing tools you can have. Think of it this way: every piece of negative feedback is a chance to turn a frustrated customer into a loyal one. By handling it with grace, transparency, and a focus on solutions, you not only fix the problem—you build lasting trust.

So, the next time you encounter negative feedback, ask yourself: how can this be an opportunity to show my audience that I'm committed to their satisfaction? What can I learn from this, and how can I turn this into a moment that strengthens, rather than weakens, my relationship with my clients? When you approach criticism with a mindset of growth and transparency, you'll find that even the most difficult situations can lead to stronger, more trusting relationships.

Chapter Takeaways

Social media has transformed how we build trust with customers. It's no longer about just posting content; it's about creating authentic relationships, showing up consistently, and being responsive. Trust isn't built overnight, and it certainly isn't built through canned responses or one-size-fits-all strategies. Instead, it's built through meaningful, transparent interactions that make your clients feel valued and heard. Whether it's engaging with influencers, handling negative feedback, or simply humanizing your brand, every interaction counts. Remember, trust on social media isn't just a tool—it's the foundation of lasting relationships.

To help solidify these lessons, here are some reflective exercises and prompts:

- **Review your social media profiles:** Do they reflect who you are and what you stand for? Are your bios, pictures, and posts aligned with the values you want to communicate to potential clients?

- **Analyze your recent content:** Have you been posting consistently, and is your content adding value to your audience? Identify areas where you can increase engagement by sharing insights, tips, or personal stories that resonate with your followers.

- **Reflect on a recent interaction:** Did you handle it authentically, or was there room to be more genuine? How can you ensure future conversations show your true intentions and commitment to your clients' needs?

- **Plan to engage with thought leaders:** Identify influencers or respected voices in your industry that you can engage with meaningfully. What steps can you take to initiate or strengthen these connections?

- **Prepare a response strategy for negative feedback:** Think through how you've handled criticism in the past. How can you improve your approach to ensure you respond promptly, professionally, and with solutions that reinforce trust?

In our next discussion, you'll see how trust, once established, becomes your most valuable asset—especially in competitive markets. What if your brand became synonymous with trust? Imagine how that could transform your reputation, relationships, and success. Let's explore deeper ways to build trust, even when competition is fierce.

Chapter 11: Building Trust in Competitive Markets

"Data is a precious thing and will last longer than the systems themselves." — Tim Berners-Lee.

What is the first thing that comes to mind when you think about building your brand in a crowded, competitive market? Is it the product features, the pricing, or maybe the marketing strategies? While all these factors are vital, there's something far more critical that often gets overlooked—you've guessed it, trust. In today's marketplace, where customers have countless options at their fingertips, what really makes your brand stand out is the level of trust you can build with your audience. Think about it: when a customer first engages with your brand, they're not just looking at what you're offering. They're evaluating whether they can trust you to deliver on your promises, stay true to your brand values, and provide a consistent experience over time. They're evaluating your factors in the trust equation. Your credibility, your reliability your intimacy, and your lack of self-orientation. So, how do you grow your brand's reputation in such a competitive space? It starts with making trust the core of your strategy.

Differentiating Through Trust

In competitive markets, it's not all about having a great product; but also consistently delivering on your promises. The businesses that thrive are the ones that show up for their customer's time and time again, exceeding expectations. I've seen countless businesses who offer a quality product or service who fail because of the lack of the basic underrated qualities that are far more attractive to customers. When you consistently deliver what you've promised—or even more—customers start to rely on you. They know they can count on you, and that kind of dependability builds trust. Think about your own experience—have you ever chosen a brand simply because you knew they wouldn't let you down, even if they weren't the cheapest or flashiest option? That's the power of consistency and reliability.

Then there's the matter of honesty in your marketing. How often do we see flashy ads that overpromise and under deliver? It may work for a quick sale, but it damages your brand's credibility in the long run. Customers want honesty. If your product isn't going to change their life overnight, don't claim that it will. For example, if you market a phone as having "all-day battery life" and it dies in four hours, customers will feel misled and lose trust. On the other hand, being upfront about your product's limitations while emphasizing its genuine strengths—such as its durability or sleek design—can earn you more respect from customers. They'll value your honesty, knowing they're getting exactly what they've been promised. This transparency builds loyalty; customers are more likely to return, not just because they liked the product, but because they trusted your brand to deliver on its word.

Building emotional connections with your customers goes beyond delivering on your promises—it's an opportunity to show that you understand and care about them. When you make an effort to know their needs, preferences, and pain points, you can offer personalized engagement that feels meaningful. Let's say you run an online bookstore. Instead of sending generic email promotions, you send tailored recommendations based on the reader's past purchases. Imagine how much more connected that customer feels to your brand compared to a mass-market company that treats everyone the same. Customers are far more likely to stick with you when you build that emotional connection.

Delivering long-term value is another key factor. As it has been made clear, it's not just about the immediate sale; it's about what happens after. Does your brand offer continuous support, product updates, or valuable resources after a customer makes a purchase? For instance, imagine a software company that not only sells a product but also offers free tutorials, webinars, and customer support long after the sale. Customers aren't just buying the software—they're buying into a relationship with a company that is genuinely invested in their success. This commitment keeps them loyal, knowing they'll continue receiving value over time.

Finally, demonstrating commitment to your clients' success is essential. It's not enough to simply close a deal. Show your customers that you're invested in their long-term outcomes by offering solutions tailored to their needs, not just what's convenient for you. A great example of this would be a consultant who spends extra time understanding a client's specific challenges before offering advice, rather than just pushing a cookie-cutter service package. When clients see that you're willing to go the extra mile, they'll know they can trust you with their future needs as well.

Navigating Price Wars with Integrity

Getting caught up in price wars is easy, especially in competitive markets. But lowering prices isn't always the best way to win customers. Instead, focus on value. Think about brands that don't compete on price, like Apple or Tesla. These companies charge premium prices, but their customers are willing to pay because they know they're getting superior quality, exceptional customer service, and an overall experience that justifies the cost. So, rather than slashing your prices, highlight the unique value you offer. Maybe it's the personalized service, the attention to detail, or the long-term benefits of your product. When you focus on what makes you different, rather than just trying to be the cheapest, you stand out.

Transparency in pricing is another key factor. Be upfront about why your prices are set the way they are. Imagine a service provider who breaks down costs for their clients, explaining the labor, materials, and expertise that go into each project. Clients feel reassured because they understand exactly what they're paying for. On the other hand, hidden fees or vague pricing structures lead to distrust and frustration. When you're open and transparent about your pricing, you show that you respect your customers and their investments.

Maintaining ethical standards, even in the heat of competition, is vital for long-term success. While cutting corners or using questionable sales tactics might win you a short-term advantage, it will inevitably damage trust in the long run. Avoid practices like adding hidden fees or pressuring customers into making decisions. Your reputation for fairness will set you apart from competitors who focus solely on short-term gains.

Rather than obsessing over price, focus on customer retention. Offering rewards for loyalty, excellent follow-up service, and personalized offers can be far more effective than a one-time discount. When customers know that they're valued beyond the initial sale, they're more likely to stay with you, even if your competitors offer lower prices. Building that long-term trust keeps your clients coming back.

Lastly, it's important to highlight your differentiators. What sets you apart from the competition? Maybe it's your product's unique features, or perhaps it's the customer testimonials and case studies that showcase your reliability. Whatever it is, ensure your clients know why you're worth the investment. When customers understand your unique value, they're less likely to be swayed by competitors offering lower prices but fewer benefits.

Trust as a Unique Selling Point

A Unique Selling Point (USP) is the key feature or advantage that sets your business apart from the competition. For some, it might be the product itself. For others, it's the service or customer experience. But trust? Trust can be the most powerful USP of all. Imagine telling your customers that while others may focus on price or flashy features, your brand is built on a foundation of trust, honesty, and reliability. That's a message that resonates deeply.

Emphasizing customer satisfaction is one of the best ways to demonstrate trust as your USP. Sharing testimonials, case studies, and feedback from happy clients can provide social proof that your brand consistently delivers. For example, an interior design firm might showcase before-and-after photos, along with client testimonials that emphasize how the designer listened to their needs and delivered beyond expectations. Prospective clients see this and think, "If they did it for them, they can do it for me too."

Creating a trust-first brand identity means making honesty, transparency, and reliability the cornerstones of everything you do —from marketing to customer service. When clients know that these values drive your business, they'll choose you over competitors who might cut corners or focus on quick wins.

Being a brand that clients trust in decision-making is a powerful advantage. When customers know they can rely on you to make the right recommendations—even if that means suggesting a competitor's product—they'll come back to you time and time again. For example, imagine a car salesperson who steers a customer toward a more affordable model because it better suits their needs, rather than pushing the most expensive option. That customer will not only buy from them, but they'll likely recommend that dealership to others because of the trust built during that experience.

Lastly, fostering long-term relationships is a surefire way to showcase trust as your USP. When you can point to long-standing client relationships, it shows new prospects that your brand is one that people stick with—because you've earned their trust over time. The value of those enduring relationships can't be overstated. Once again, trust isn't about making a sale today; it's about building partnerships that last for years and sales to come.

Chapter Takeaways

Trust in competitive markets isn't just an advantage—it's essential. It's the factor that differentiates you from the competition, keeps your customers loyal, and turns transactions into long-term relationships. When you build trust through consistency, honesty, and a genuine commitment to your client's success, you create a foundation that can withstand the pressures of competition. Think about it—would you rather compete on price, or stand out as the brand that clients can rely on? Trust gives you that edge.

As you reflect on this chapter, ask yourself: How are you building trust in your own competitive market? Are you focusing on delivering long-term value, or are you caught up in the race to the bottom with pricing wars? Have you positioned trust as your unique selling point, or are you blending in with the crowd?

Here are some exercises to help you implement the ideas from this chapter:

- **Evaluate Your Brand's Consistency**: Reflect on whether you consistently deliver on your promises. Where have you met or exceeded expectations, and where can you improve? What steps can you take to ensure that every customer experience aligns with your brand values?

- **Audit Your Marketing for Honesty**: Review your latest marketing campaigns. Are you making claims you can deliver on, or are there areas where you might be overpromising? How can you adjust your messaging to ensure transparency and authenticity?

- **Personalize Your Client Engagement**: Think about a few recent client interactions. Did you take the time to understand their unique needs and pain points, or did you offer a one-size-fits-all solution? Make a plan to personalize your approach for each client moving forward, ensuring that you're addressing their specific challenges and not just offering generic solutions.

- **Analyze Your Pricing Structure for Transparency**: Are you clear about how you price your products or services? Take a moment to review your pricing and consider how you can be more transparent with your clients. Can you offer a breakdown of costs or explain the value they're getting in a way that builds trust?

- **Highlight Your Differentiators**: Identify three things that set you apart from your competitors. Are you effectively communicating these differentiators to your clients? How can you make these points of difference more central to your sales process to build deeper trust with your audience?

Now, as you think about building trust as your unique selling point, consider how you can leverage that trust to not only differentiate your brand but also maintain it in the long run. Ask yourself: What would your business look like if trust was the cornerstone of every interaction, every marketing campaign, and every customer service moment?

In our next discussion, we'll explore how you can use data and analytics to build even deeper levels of trust with your clients. After all, in today's world, information is power, and the way you use that information can either build trust or destroy it.

Chapter 12: Leveraging Data and Analytics to Build Trust

"The goal is to turn data into information, and information into insight." — Carly Fiorina.

In today's digital landscape, data is not just a tool—it's the backbone of any successful business strategy. But with great power comes great responsibility, especially when it comes to handling customer data. Have you ever wondered how the data you collect influences your relationship with your customers? It's one thing to gather information about preferences, behaviors, and past interactions, but it's another thing entirely to use that data in a way that fosters trust. As businesses grow and access to data becomes more sophisticated, the need for transparency, security, and personalization has never been more important. Building trust is a far more extended responsibility than just your interaction with clients. It reaches into all intricate details of business including the information that your clients entrust to you. So, how do you ensure that the data you collect is working in your favor, building bridges rather than walls?

Let's start with transparency. Imagine you're the customer for a moment. How would you feel if you suddenly noticed that a company was sending you hyper-personalized recommendations without any clear explanation of how they got your data? Suspicious, right? That's why it's crucial to let your clients know exactly what data you're collecting and, more importantly, how it benefits them. People are much more likely to share their information when they understand the reason behind it and feel in control. A simple, upfront message like, "We use your browsing habits to offer you tailored product recommendations," can make all the difference in how a customer perceives your use of their data. Without this clarity, even the most well-meaning personalization efforts can feel invasive rather than helpful.

But transparency alone isn't enough. You need to pair it with a solid commitment to data protection. We've all heard horror stories of data breaches and the fallout that follows. When personal information is exposed, it doesn't just result in financial loss for businesses—it results in a loss of trust, which can be far more difficult to recover. Have you ever hesitated to make a purchase or sign up for a service because you weren't sure your data would be secure? That hesitation is exactly what you need to address proactively with your customers. By implementing stringent security protocols—like encryption and regular system audits—you signal to your clients that their data is in safe hands. And don't forget to communicate this to them. A statement as simple as, "Your privacy is our priority. We've implemented industry-leading security measures to protect your information," can ease concerns and strengthen trust.

Let's talk about why you're collecting that data in the first place. If your clients share their personal information with you, they want to know, "What's in it for me?" And rightly so. The best way to use data responsibly is to show clients that it directly benefits them. Imagine a customer who frequently purchases a specific type of product from your business. If they receive a personalized email offering a discount on that item, they'll appreciate that you're paying attention to their needs. When done right, personalization becomes more than a marketing tactic—it becomes a way easier to show customers that you care about what matters to them. Even though using data can increase the sales you make, it's important to keep in mind that's it's also used to enhance the customer experience in a thoughtful and considerate way.

And while we're on the topic of responsibility, let's not forget about the legal side of things. With laws like the General Data Protection Regulation (GDPR) shaping how businesses handle data, it's vital to ensure that your practices are compliant. Why does this matter to your clients? Because to them, they don't care what the legal requirements are. If they did, people would be conducting due diligence all of the time. They see your legal compliance as a reflection of your commitment to doing things the right way. When you communicate that your data collection is in line with industry regulations; you're telling your customers, "We respect your privacy and follow strict guidelines to protect your data." This shows that your brand values integrity, which goes a long way in building trust.

Finally, giving customers control over their data is an empowering way to build that trust. People want to feel that they're not just data points to be harvested—they want to know they have a say in how their information is used. Have you ever appreciated a company giving you the option to manage your preferences or opt out of certain data practices? It feels empowering, doesn't it? When you allow customers to adjust their data preferences or choose how much information they share, you show that you respect their autonomy. This kind of transparency fosters a deeper sense of trust because clients know they are not being forced into something—they have control over what's theirs.

In the end, how you handle customer data speaks volumes about your values as a business. By using data responsibly, transparently, and with the customer's best interest in mind, you're not just meeting expectations but exceeding them. When clients know that their data is safe, that it's being used to enhance their experience, and that they're in control, you're creating the perfect conditions for trust to flourish.

Building Trust through Personalization

We've touched on personalization a few times, but now it's time to really explore how it can elevate your customer relationships. We know that personalization goes beyond simply addressing someone by name or sending a cookie-cutter promotional email. It's about showing that you genuinely understand your customers—their needs, interests, preferences—and using that knowledge to enhance their experience in meaningful and thoughtful ways. But let's be honest: have you ever received a "personalized" message that felt anything but? The kind of email that slaps your name at the top but offers something irrelevant? That's exactly what you want to avoid.

Imagine running an online store and noticing a customer frequently buys from a particular category. Instead of blasting them with a generic newsletter covering all your product offerings, why not narrow your focus? Send them a message highlighting the latest arrivals in that specific category, with a subject line like, "We thought you'd love these new picks based on your recent purchases." That subtle nod to their past behavior can be incredibly engaging. It's a small gesture, but one that tells the customer, "Hey, we see you. We get what you're into, and we're making this easier for you."

Now, let's think about sales pitches. Personalization here is way more than knowing a customer's name but really understanding who they are, and what they really need as a solution to their problems. What will truly resonate with them? Maybe they've been browsing specific product features on your website or asked questions about certain services in the past. Armed with that data, you can focus your pitch on what you know will matter most to them, without overwhelming them with irrelevant details. But there's a fine line—have you ever felt like a company knew a little *too* much about you? That's where balance comes into play. You want to show customers that you've paid attention without making them feel like they're being watched too closely. It's the difference between being attentive and being invasive.

Another powerful tool in your personalization toolbox is audience segmentation. Think of your customer base as a diverse group with different interests and motivations. Some customers might be more drawn to premium services, while others are looking for the best deal. Instead of treating everyone the same, segment your audience based on factors like purchasing behavior, location, or even how often they engage with your brand. If you've ever received a tailored message that seemed to speak directly to your specific interests, you've experienced the power of segmentation firsthand. It's like having a conversation that feels personal, rather than hearing a sales pitch aimed at everyone and no one at the same time.

But here's where things can go sideways: personalization that doesn't add value can backfire. Imagine getting a "personalized" offer for something you've never shown interest in—it's not just annoying; it can actually damage trust. So always ask yourself: "Is this message truly relevant to my customer?" If the answer is no, then it's better not to send it. Customers can sense when personalization feels forced or insincere, and when that happens, it doesn't build trust—it breaks it.

Chapter Takeaways

Leveraging data responsibly is about building trust at every touchpoint. Trust grows naturally when your clients see that you respect their data, keep it secure, and use it to enhance their experience. Think of data not just as numbers, but as insights that allow you to personalize, protect, and empower your customers. Using data wisely creates an environment where trust becomes a natural part of your relationship with every client.

Reflect on these prompts and ask yourself how well your current data practices foster trust:

- **Evaluate Your Transparency:** How clear are you about the data you collect and how it's used? Take a look at your communication strategies and see where you can make them more transparent.

- **Security Check:** When was the last time you audited your data security measures? Consider implementing stronger protection protocols and sharing these efforts with your customers.

- **Customer Empowerment:** Are you giving your clients control over their data? Explore ways to offer more opt-out options or ways for clients to manage their preferences.

- **Personalization with Purpose:** Review your personalization efforts. Are they genuinely adding value for your customers, or do they feel superficial? Adjust your strategy to ensure your personalization efforts build trust.

- **Clear Communication:** Is your privacy policy understandable and easy to find? Revisit how you present it to ensure it's as straightforward and accessible as possible.

As we move forward, think about the internal trust that drives your business. How do your teams work together to maintain the high standards of trust you've set with your clients? Next, we'll delve deeper into the trust that exists between your sales teams and internal stakeholders—an essential component for long-term success.

Trust within your organization is just as vital as the trust you build with your clients. When your sales team, marketing, and operations all align around the same principles of transparency, reliability, and shared goals, your external trust-building efforts become even more powerful. But how does that internal trust develop? What role does communication, accountability, and leadership play in creating an environment where everyone works towards a common purpose? In the next discussion, we'll explore these internal dynamics, understanding how the relationships between your sales teams and internal stakeholders can shape the long-term success and integrity of your business.

Ask yourself this: How strong are the relationships within your team, and how does that internal trust impact your ability to serve your clients? Understanding this connection could be the key to unlocking even greater success in your organization.

Chapter 13: Trust Between Sales Teams and Internal Stakeholders

"The speed of trust is the difference between a thriving business and a struggling one."— Stephen M.R. Covey.

Have you ever been in a workplace where communication is fragmented, and team members are left guessing about their roles? Or maybe you've experienced the frustration of working in an environment where internal competition outweighs collaboration. In those moments, it's clear that trust—between colleagues, departments, and leadership—isn't just a nice-to-have; it's imperative for the health and success of the organization. Without it, even the best sales strategies can fall flat. Building and maintaining trust within an organization is the foundation for a productive, collaborative, and thriving business. But how do you foster that trust, and more importantly, how do you ensure it's not only established but sustained across all levels of the organization?

Internal Trust Building

The cornerstone of internal trust is **transparency in communication**. Whether it's between sales teams, management, or support departments, open and honest communication fosters a sense of reliability and mutual respect. When communication breaks down, assumptions start to take root, and that's when mistrust creeps in. Imagine a sales team that isn't clear on the goals set by leadership, or support teams that aren't aligned with the sales strategies. The result? Missed targets, unhappy clients, and team frustration. Transparency clears up confusion and ensures everyone works toward the same goal.

Another key aspect of building trust is **encouraging feedback loops**. Have you ever worked somewhere where feedback only went one way—top-down? That can quickly create resentment and break down trust. Just as clients want to be heard, so do the people within your organization. Particularly when things go south. Instead, fostering a culture where feedback is a two-way street—both from leadership to team members and from team members back to leadership—promotes a collaborative, trusting environment. For example, consider an organization that holds regular feedback sessions where team members openly share their thoughts on process improvements and management decisions. This kind of culture encourages mutual respect and continuous growth because everyone feels heard. When feedback is valued and acted upon, trust strengthens naturally.

Collaborative decision-making also plays a critical role in building internal trust. When all stakeholders, including sales teams, marketing, and customer service, are involved in decision-making, they feel ownership over the process. That sense of ownership is crucial for building a culture of trust. Let's consider an example from a real-life study involving engineering design teams in China. The study found that when teams practiced shared leadership—where decision-making is distributed among team members rather than dictated solely from the top—they saw a significant boost in team effectiveness.

In this study, 26 teams with 119 individuals participated, and the findings highlighted how shared leadership positively influenced team task performance and overall team viability. By engaging all members in the decision-making process, teams were able to harness diverse perspectives, which led to more creative solutions and better outcomes. Imagine the difference between a company where leadership makes all the decisions versus one where sales teams are actively invited to contribute their insights. The latter not only empowers team members but also enhances collaboration, job satisfaction, and overall team cohesion.

The research further showed that shared leadership was particularly effective in the early phases of projects. When teams collaborated early on, they were able to generate more innovative strategies and plan effectively for later stages, resulting in smoother execution down the line. For project managers and organizational leaders, this insight emphasizes the value of involving team members from the start, allowing them to share their expertise and influence key decisions.

Bringing this back to your organization: if you're only involving leadership in strategic decisions without consulting your team, you risk creating a disconnect. But when teams are asked for their input and given a voice, they become more invested in the outcome. This approach builds a sense of belonging and accountability, which in turn fuels trust and drives better performance.

Having **clear roles and expectations** is another often overlooked trust-building tool. When everyone on the team knows exactly what's expected of them, it reduces confusion and ensures accountability. There's no finger-pointing or blaming because each person understands their responsibilities and how they fit into the bigger picture. Think about the last time you were unsure of your role in a project—didn't it create uncertainty and stress? Now imagine the clarity and confidence you'd feel knowing exactly what's expected. That's the kind of environment that limits conflict and fosters trust.

And finally, it's essential to **recognize and reward trustworthy behavior**. When team members consistently act with integrity, show reliability, and demonstrate transparency, it's important to acknowledge that. Recognition, whether through awards, bonuses, or even a simple thank you, reinforces trust across the team. People want to know their efforts are seen and valued. A team that feels recognized for its trustworthy behavior will continue to invest in fostering those positive traits, creating a ripple effect throughout the organization.

Collaborative Selling

When it comes to collaborative selling, trust between team members becomes even more important. It's not enough for one salesperson to do their job well—every person involved in the sales process must trust that their colleagues will fulfill their roles effectively. Trust among team members ensures that everyone can confidently rely on each other's expertise, whether it's the marketing department generating quality leads, the sales team closing deals, or the customer service team ensuring client satisfaction post-sale. Without this internal trust, cracks appear, which can lead to lost sales opportunities or a disjointed customer experience.

In a truly collaborative environment, cross-departmental trust is essential. Sales, marketing, and customer service teams must work together seamlessly to provide a cohesive customer experience. Have you ever dealt with a company where it felt like one hand didn't know what the other was doing? Maybe the marketing team promised something the sales team couldn't deliver, or customer service had no idea what the client was sold. That lack of trust between departments can erode customer confidence. However, when all teams are aligned, the customer experience is smooth and professional, which builds trust internally and extends that trust to clients.

To address the challenge of miscommunication and improve collaboration, several strategies can be implemented:

1. **Implement a Centralized Communication Platform**: Using a unified platform like Slack, Microsoft Teams, or Asana can streamline communication and reduce the chaos that often comes with multiple channels. These tools allow for real-time collaboration, easy file sharing, and centralized updates. By ensuring that everyone has access to the same information, it becomes easier to respond quickly and keep all teams on the same page. This helps eliminate the confusion and delays often caused by traditional email chains.

2. **Encourage Cross-Departmental Collaboration and Regular Meetings**: Scheduling regular interdepartmental meetings fosters open dialogue and builds relationships between teams. Cross-functional teams working on shared projects can align their goals, provide updates, and address issues collaboratively. For instance, imagine a scenario where the marketing team, sales team, and customer service team come together weekly to discuss current campaigns, lead quality, and client feedback. This proactive approach helps ensure that everyone is aware of the ongoing work and any potential challenges, leading to smoother workflows and fewer misunderstandings.

3. **Establish Clear Communication Protocols and Roles**: Defining specific communication protocols—such as who is responsible for updates, how information should be shared, and when—ensures clarity and efficiency. This structure makes certain that the right people are informed, and important messages don't get lost in the shuffle. When roles are clearly outlined, team members know exactly who

to turn to for answers or decisions, minimizing delays and enhancing trust. A consistent process avoids unnecessary back-and-forth and helps teams move faster and with more confidence.

Another essential aspect is fostering a culture of **shared responsibility for success**. In a competitive environment, it's easy for team members to start competing against one another instead of working together. But when success is shared and everyone has a stake in the outcome, it promotes trust and reduces internal competition. Think about a project where everyone is pulling in the same direction—doesn't it create a sense of unity and trust? When each team member feels responsible for the overall success, it strengthens internal trust and drives better results.

Lastly, training for collaborative skills is key. Building trust requires effort, and that includes investing in team-building and collaboration training. These initiatives help strengthen relationships, encourage open communication, and build trust among team members, which is critical for a high-functioning, collaborative sales environment.

Maintaining Trust in Sales Leadership

When it comes to maintaining trust in sales leadership, the most important thing a leader can do is **lead by example**. Sales leaders set the tone for the rest of the team, and their actions are constantly being watched. Leaders who demonstrate transparency, reliability, and accountability inspire trust in their teams. Think of a sales leader who regularly communicates openly with their team, follows through on promises, and admits when they've made mistakes. That kind of leadership earns trust and encourages the team to emulate those behaviors.

Clear communication of goals is another critical factor. Teams need to know exactly what they're working toward and why. If goals are vague or inconsistent, it creates confusion and uncertainty, which can diminish trust. However, when leaders clearly articulate the team's objectives and the strategy to achieve them, it builds trust by showing that the leadership has a clear plan and that everyone is working together toward the same outcome.

Leaders who **empower their team members** build a deeper sense of trust also. Empowerment means giving team members the autonomy to make decisions, take ownership of their roles, and be accountable for their actions. No one likes to be micromanaged, and when leaders trust their teams enough to give them independence, it fosters mutual trust. Think about the last time you were given full ownership of a task or project—didn't it make you feel more invested in the outcome? That's the influence of empowerment in building trust.

Another key aspect is **consistency in decision-making**. Leaders making fair, consistent decisions creates a sense of security within the team. People trust leaders who are predictable and fair because they know what to expect. Have you ever worked for a leader whose decisions seemed arbitrary or inconsistent? It can lead to anxiety and mistrust. But when decisions are made fairly and consistently, trust flourishes.

Finally, **regular check-ins and support** are crucial for building and maintaining trust in leadership. Providing regular feedback, offering guidance, and being available to help team members when needed shows that leaders are invested in the success of the team. It reinforces the idea that leadership isn't just about giving orders but supporting and guiding the team toward success. One goal of successful leadership is to make your team feel like they're in good hands. Similar to how consistent effort shows clients that you care about them and want to gain their trust, being a leader with these consistent qualities will make your team want to work for you and achieve great success with you.

One of the primary goals of effective leadership is to make your team feel confident and secure, knowing they are in capable hands. When leaders demonstrate a consistent commitment to their team—just as you would with clients—it shows that they genuinely care about each member's growth and success. This sense of security and dedication motivates the team to work harder, not just for themselves but for the leader who they trust and respect. When team members see that you're invested in their progress, they become more committed to working alongside you, striving to achieve success together as a united force. This collaborative trust and mutual respect become the foundation for long-term success and a thriving work environment.

Chapter Takeaways

Trust within an organization isn't built overnight, but it's the cornerstone of a thriving, collaborative business. Whether it's through transparent communication, shared decision-making, or empowering team members, internal trust forms the foundation for a seamless, high-functioning team. Leaders who lead by example, foster open feedback, and consistently support their teams create an environment where trust can flourish. When internal trust is strong, it extends outward, creating a ripple effect that impacts everything from sales success to client satisfaction.

Now, let's reflect on how you can start implementing trust-building strategies within your organization:

- Take a moment to assess the transparency of your communication. Are you fostering an environment where open dialogue is encouraged across departments?

- Review your feedback systems. Are they two-way, allowing not just top-down feedback but also input from team members? How can you improve this?
- Think about the decision-making process within your team. Are all relevant stakeholders involved? How can you make the process more inclusive to build a sense of ownership?
- Consider the clarity of roles within your team. Is there confusion about who's responsible for what? How can you create more clarity and accountability?
- Reflect on how often you recognize and reward trustworthy behavior. How can you make trust a celebrated value within your organization?

As you think about these strategies, start picturing what your organization could achieve with deeper trust woven into every layer. Our next discussion will explore how cultural sensitivity is critical in building trust, especially in global sales environments.

Chapter 14: Cultural Sensitivity and Trust in Global Sales

"In a global marketplace, trust is built by understanding and respecting cultural differences." — Unknown.

Have you ever found yourself in a business situation where everything seemed aligned, but the deal fell through simply because there was a cultural disconnect? It's not uncommon. In a global marketplace, the tactics that cultivate trust can be very advantageous, but there is a new aspect that becomes relevant. That is understanding the nuances of different cultures and adapting your approach to meet those expectations. Cultural sensitivity in global sales is about fostering genuine connections that transcend borders and create a solid foundation of trust. By recognizing and respecting cultural differences, you avoid misunderstandings and demonstrate that you value your clients' unique perspectives and practices. This is how true trust is built in the global business arena.

Understanding Cultural Norms

Each culture has its own unique way of building trust and conducting business, and these variations are crucial for any professional engaging in international sales to understand. In some parts of the globe, trust is cemented through formal contracts and clear agreements, establishing a sense of security from the outset. In other regions, however, personal relationships and informal communication carry more weight. Imagine entering a meeting fully prepared with detailed contracts, only to find that your potential clients are more interested in having a meal together and discussing family or local events first. In these cultures, that personal connection is often as important—if not more so—than the business deal itself. Being attuned to these subtleties helps you navigate these environments more effectively, avoiding misunderstandings that can hinder progress.

Hierarchy and protocol are also essential aspects to consider. In many cultures, such as those in East Asia, respecting the hierarchy is fundamental. Decisions are often made by senior leaders, and bypassing this structure can be perceived as disrespectful. For instance, if you're working in a country where seniority is highly valued, and you approach someone lower in the organizational chain before speaking with a key decision-maker, it could be interpreted as dismissing the importance of their business structure. This simple misstep can create a barrier to trust that might take considerable effort to overcome.

In relationship-focused cultures, like those found in Asia and Latin America, patience and multiple interactions are essential for building trust. Unlike transactional cultures in Northern Europe or the U.S., where trust can be established quickly if the terms are clear, these relationship-based environments require time and engagement. For example, while a well-crafted proposal might suffice in a transactional setting, building rapport over several meetings is often necessary elsewhere. Being flexible enough to adapt your approach to fit these varying cultural contexts is a vital skill in international sales.

Building personal rapport before diving into business is not merely a polite gesture in many cultures; it is often a requirement. Discussing family, hobbies, or local customs can help open doors that might otherwise remain closed. If you rush into business discussions without establishing that personal connection first, clients may hesitate or become resistant. But if you take the time to engage on a personal level, you create a sense of familiarity and comfort that paves the way for a smoother, more productive business relationship. For instance, sharing a genuine interest in their culture, hobbies, or local events can show that you're invested beyond just the deal itself, which naturally builds trust.

Respecting local customs is another critical element when engaging in cross-cultural interactions. Small gestures, like knowing the appropriate way to greet someone or understanding the significance of gift-giving, can make a big difference. For example, in Japan, the exchange of business cards is not just a formality; it's an important ritual that shows respect. Presenting and receiving a business card with both hands and making a slight bow demonstrates that you value their business culture, boosting trust right from the start. Conversely, missteps like offering an inappropriate gift or ignoring dining etiquette can create unnecessary barriers, damaging trust and making it difficult to recover.

With Preparation

To ensure successful cross-cultural interactions, preparation is key. This involves not only understanding the cultural landscape but also seeking insights from credible resources.

- **Research Country-Specific Cultural Etiquette:** Before engaging with clients from different cultures, consult resources such as Hofstede Insights, *The Culture Map*, or books on international business etiquette. These guides provide a detailed overview of cultural dimensions like power distance (the importance of hierarchy), individualism vs. collectivism, and how different cultures manage uncertainty. For instance, Hofstede's analysis of Latin American countries highlights their strong emphasis on relationships and group decision-making. This insight suggests that, in these regions, building a personal connection before delving into business is vital.

- **Leverage Past Experiences and Local Experts:** First-hand experiences can provide valuable, nuanced information that books may not cover. Engaging with colleagues or business partners who have worked in a particular country can reveal specific customs or industry expectations. For example, if you have a colleague familiar with South Korea, they might emphasize the importance of formal greetings and using titles correctly, helping you navigate initial meetings respectfully.

- **Study Cultural Business Protocols:** Look for reports or online resources outlining business protocols such as meeting etiquette, dress codes, and communication preferences. For example, in Germany, a formal approach is expected in business interactions, while in Australia, things might be more laid back. In Japan, the way you present a business card—holding it with both hands and bowing slightly—signifies respect for titles and hierarchy.

On the Spot

Even with extensive preparation, being observant and adaptable in real-time is just as important when navigating cultural interactions.

- **Observe Meeting Structure and Interactions:** Pay close attention to the structure of the meeting. Does it start with formalities, or is it casual? Understanding whether the focus is initially on relationships or directly on business provides insight into what is valued in that culture. For example, if a Middle Eastern client spends considerable time discussing personal matters or showing hospitality, it signals that relationship-building is prioritized before any business can proceed. Recognizing and adapting to these cues will help you fit in smoothly.

- **Pick Up on Body Language and Nonverbal Cues:** Nonverbal communication often speaks louder than words. For instance, maintaining eye contact is considered a sign of confidence in the U.S., but in Japan, it may be perceived as too forward. Similarly, the acceptable physical distance varies—while Latin American cultures may be comfortable with closer proximity, Nordic cultures might prefer more space. Understanding these subtleties allows you to adjust your approach accordingly, ensuring your body language aligns with local expectations.

- **Listen for Directness or Indirectness in Speech:** Communication styles also vary significantly. Cultures like the Dutch or Germans value directness and clarity, while many Asian cultures favor a more indirect approach to maintain harmony and avoid confrontation. For example, if a client seems hesitant or avoids strong language, it might indicate a preference for diplomatic communication. Adapting your response to this indirect style demonstrates that you respect their cultural norms, enhancing trust.

By blending preparation and real-time observation, you create a comprehensive strategy for building trust across diverse cultural landscapes. Adaptability is an invaluable skill which is an essential part of fostering strong business relationships in international contexts. The more you align yourself with the cultural norms and expectations of your clients, the more effectively you build lasting and meaningful trust.

Adapting Communication Styles

When dealing with clients across different cultures, your communication style matters immensely. What works in one region might be seen as overly direct or too subtle in another. To truly build trust, you need to adapt the way you communicate based on cultural preferences. Your communication style is not only about language but also about tone, body language, and the underlying context of the conversation. Every interaction carries meaning beyond the words themselves, and being able to navigate these nuances can significantly strengthen the trust you build with your clients.

Here's how you can adapt your communication style across different cultural contexts:

- **Direct vs. Indirect Communication**
  In some cultures, like the U.S. and Germany, direct communication is not only appreciated but expected. People from these cultures value straightforwardness and clarity. They want you to get to the point, make your argument, and leave little room for ambiguity. For instance, when pitching a product, it's effective to clearly outline the benefits, explain the price, and directly ask for the sale. Anything less might come across as evasive or even dishonest. However, in other cultures, such as Japan or India, communication can be much more indirect. Here, people may prefer to imply their meaning rather than state it outright, especially if they think the truth might cause discomfort. In these contexts, being overly blunt can be seen as disrespectful or even aggressive. When dealing with clients from such cultures, you may need to adopt a more subtle approach, where the message is gently woven into the conversation, allowing your client to "read between the lines" without feeling pressured. This adjustment is crucial

because failing to recognize these preferences can lead to misunderstandings or even damage trust.

- **Tone and Body Language**
  Words only make up a part of the message. The rest is conveyed through tone and body language, and this can vary dramatic between cultures. In many East Asian cultures, such as in South Korea, a calm, measured tone is not only preferred but seen as a sign of respect. Raising your voice, gesturing excessively, or showing strong emotions can be interpreted as a lack of control, which can erode trust. On the other hand, in cultures like Italy or Brazil, a more expressive communication style is often embraced. People might use their hands more, engage in animated discussions, and expect the same from you. Being too reserved in these settings could be taken as a sign of indifference or a lack of enthusiasm. The challenge lies in reading the room and adjusting your energy levels accordingly. A calm, respectful demeanor in one culture might need to be balanced with more dynamic engagement in another. It's about understanding and mirroring cultural preferences in a way that feels authentic to both parties.

- **Understanding Time Perception**
  Time can be viewed very differently across cultures. In places like the U.S. or Germany, time is often treated as a finite resource—punctuality is prized, deadlines are sacred, and efficiency is key. Meetings are expected to start and end on time, and getting straight to business is the norm. In these cultures, being even a few minutes late without explanation can dismantle trust, as it may be interpreted as a sign of disrespect or disorganization. On the other hand, in many Middle Eastern or African cultures, time can be seen as more fluid. There's often less urgency to stick rigidly to schedules, and social interactions may take

precedence over strict timelines. If you rush through a meeting or push too hard to stick to a tight schedule, you may come across as impatient or dismissive of the relationship-building process. Understanding these differences allows you to manage expectations better, showing that you respect the cultural norms around time. Being patient and flexible when necessary can strengthen trust and demonstrate your willingness to adapt to the client's pace.

- **Using Local Languages or Dialects**
  While English is widely spoken in global business, making an effort to speak your client's language—or at least understanding some key phrases—can dramatically enhance trust. For example, if you're conducting business in China, learning a few basic greetings or phrases in Mandarin, even if the meeting is conducted in English, shows respect and a genuine interest in the culture. It's a small gesture but goes a long way in establishing rapport. Imagine how you would feel if someone from another country came to you and made the effort to greet you in your own language. It's a sign that they respect where you come from and aren't just treating you like any other business partner. This effort to bridge the linguistic gap signals that you're willing to meet your client halfway, building a foundation of mutual respect. Even if you make mistakes, the effort alone often earns you goodwill and opens the door to a more trusting relationship.

- **Respecting Communication Preferences**
  Different cultures have different preferences when it comes to how they communicate, and failing to adapt to these preferences can lead to miscommunication or frustration. For example, in some cultures, like those in Northern Europe, written communication—such as emails—may be

the preferred mode of professional interaction. People expect well-thought-out, detailed emails outlining key points and decisions. Face-to-face meetings might be reserved for more significant discussions. In contrast, many Asian or Middle Eastern cultures place higher value on personal interactions, preferring in-person meetings or phone calls over written correspondence. These cultures may see written communication as too impersonal for building trust, especially at the start of a relationship. Understanding these preferences ensures that you're not only delivering your message but doing so in a way that resonates with the client. For example, if your client prefers face-to-face meetings, suggesting a quick phone call might seem dismissive. On the other hand, if they value concise emails, overloading them with too many calls or meetings could feel like an unnecessary imposition. Adjusting how you communicate based on these cultural preferences signals that you're listening to what matters to them.

In global sales, trust is built on the foundation of effective, respectful communication. Adapting your style to meet the expectations of your clients shows that you're not just interested in closing the deal but are genuinely invested in understanding and valuing their perspective. This commitment to meeting them where they are is what builds long-term, trust-filled relationships that transcend cultural barriers.

Ethical Sales Practices in Global Markets

Operating in global markets demands a high level of ethical responsibility. Different countries have varying regulations, expectations, and ethical standards, and being well-versed in these is essential for building trust. Understanding the legal landscape is more than a requirement—it's a commitment to show your clients that you're reliable and conscientious. Let's explore how being proactive about navigating local regulations sets the foundation for ethical, trust-based business practices.

Every country has its own set of rules governing how businesses operate, particularly regarding sales practices, advertising, and data protection. Ignoring these regulations isn't just a legal risk—it can significantly damage your credibility and relationships with clients. Imagine expanding your business into a region with strict privacy laws like the General Data Protection Regulation (GDPR) in Europe. If you fail to comply with these regulations, you risk hefty fines and the trust of your clients. In the e-commerce industry, for instance, companies that transparently communicate how they handle customer data and the steps they take to comply with local laws are much more likely to earn client trust. This proactive approach shows that you're not only aiming for short-term profits but are committed to building a responsible and sustainable relationship with the market.

To navigate local regulations effectively, start by consulting official government and trade websites. Many countries have portals like the U.S. Department of Commerce or UK Trade and Investment, which provide comprehensive legal guides for doing business within their jurisdictions. For businesses targeting the European market, the European Commission offers invaluable resources on GDPR and other regulatory frameworks, ensuring you have the most up-to-date information before you make any moves. These government resources serve as a reliable first step in understanding the regulatory environment you're entering.

Beyond initial research, it's also crucial to gain insight into the legal environment regarding anti-corruption and bribery laws. Organizations such as Transparency International or the OECD provide detailed, country-specific information that can guide your business practices. Transparency International's Corruption Perceptions Index, for example, ranks countries based on perceived corruption levels, highlighting regions where you may need to exercise extra caution. Having this knowledge allows you to develop compliance strategies tailored to specific markets, ensuring you maintain ethical practices wherever you operate.

But there's no substitute for on-the-ground expertise. Consulting local legal experts can help you navigate complex and nuanced regulations, especially in countries with stringent anti-bribery laws like the U.S. or the UK. Firms like Baker McKenzie or DLA Piper specialize in international business law and provide tailored advice that aligns with local regulations. Collaborating with such experts demonstrates to your clients that you are committed to following the rules and making informed, ethical decisions that protect their interests as well as your own. This extra step goes a long way in building a reputation as a trustworthy and law-abiding partner.

Transparency in cross-cultural negotiations is another critical component of ethical sales practices. The expectation for openness and honesty in business dealings varies across cultures. In some places, business partners expect every detail laid out upfront, while in others, indirect communication is more common. Regardless of the cultural context, maintaining transparency about what you can deliver and any limitations is key. Imagine negotiating with a partner in Japan, a country that values long-term relationships and mutual respect. If you overpromise or fail to meet your commitments, you risk damaging your reputation beyond repair. Clients appreciate honesty, even when it means admitting you can't deliver everything they might want. It's better to acknowledge potential limitations early on, showing that you're a transparent and reliable partner, which builds long-term trust and may lead to future opportunities even if the initial deal doesn't materialize.

Respecting anti-corruption practices and bribery laws is also essential in building trust. While some countries might culturally accept small gifts or "facilitation fees" as part of doing business, these actions can be illegal in others, particularly in Western markets where anti-corruption laws are strict. For example, the U.S. Foreign Corrupt Practices Act (FCPA) strictly prohibits U.S. businesses from offering bribes to foreign officials, even if such practices are culturally acceptable abroad. Something as seemingly benign as a high-value gift could be seen as unethical or unlawful. Consulting anti-corruption organizations like Transparency International ensures you are aware of these differences, helping you avoid legal pitfalls while demonstrating to your clients that your focus is on long-term, ethical practices rather than quick, questionable wins.

Another critical element in maintaining trust is adhering to fair trade practices and ethical sourcing. In global markets where corporate social responsibility (CSR) is a key concern, clients and consumers often judge brands based on their commitment to ethical standards. Take the fashion industry, for example, where increasing demand for transparency in sourcing and labor practices affects buying decisions. Brands that can prove they adhere to ethical sourcing practices, treat their workers fairly, and employ sustainable methods naturally earn stronger trust with their clientele. If your business can communicate its commitment to these values—whether in manufacturing, tech, or any other sector—clients are more likely to view you as a trustworthy and responsible partner.

Cultural sensitivity in marketing also plays a significant role in how your business is perceived globally. Campaigns that fail to consider local customs and values can severely damage trust. A single mistake—like using culturally insensitive imagery or language—can quickly go viral and tarnish your brand's image. For example, entering the Middle Eastern market without understanding local norms could lead to an ad campaign that offends societal values, potentially resulting in boycotts or long-term damage to your reputation. On the flip side, companies that invest the time to understand and respect the cultural nuances of their target markets demonstrate care and consideration, which fosters deeper trust. This shows clients that your company values cultural awareness and is not simply applying a one-size-fits-all strategy.

To ensure that your marketing campaigns align with cultural expectations, preparation is key. Utilizing market research tools like Google Trends, Statista, or Nielsen can offer insights into consumer behavior patterns specific to the regions you're targeting. These tools help you understand what's currently trending in a country, allowing you to tailor your message accordingly. For example, using Google Trends to see what's popular in India might help you align your campaign with current interests, positioning your brand as relevant and attentive. Such a proactive approach reflects cultural awareness and shows that you're committed to connecting authentically with your audience.

Another strategy is to consult cultural marketing guides and online resources that offer guidance on how to adapt advertisements, messaging, and even visual elements like color schemes. It's important to recognize that while one color might symbolize luck in one culture, it could convey an entirely different message elsewhere. For instance, red is seen as a lucky color in Chinese culture but may signify danger in many Western contexts. Understanding these nuances helps you create campaigns that are not only effective but respectful, reinforcing your commitment to being a responsible global brand.

Observing customer reactions and engagement is another critical step once your campaign is live. If you notice low engagement or negative responses, it might indicate that the message isn't resonating culturally. This feedback allows you to adjust your campaign, demonstrating that you are responsive and respectful of the audience's values. By doing so, you can rebuild and strengthen trust even when things don't go as planned.

Finally, looking at local competitors or successful international brands can offer a wealth of information. Coca-Cola, for instance, is known for its localized campaigns, which reflect cultural nuances that resonate with local audiences. In India, the brand often features Bollywood celebrities and ties its advertisements to festivals like Diwali, making the brand feel familiar and culturally aligned. Studying such successful campaigns helps you understand what works in different markets, allowing you to refine your approach and connect with your audience on a deeper level.

Chapter Takeaways

Building trust in global sales requires more than just knowledge of your product or market; it demands a deep understanding and respect for the cultural dynamics that shape how business is conducted across different regions. Think about it this way: when you step into a new market, you're not just offering a product or service, you're entering a complex web of cultural values, social norms, and expectations. How you navigate these differences will determine whether you build lasting relationships or stumble into misunderstandings. Cultural sensitivity, therefore, is not merely a tactic—it's a core philosophy that signals to your clients that you see them as more than numbers on a balance sheet. When you make the effort to understand their world, you demonstrate that you're genuinely invested in their success, and that kind of trust is unshakable.

So, how can you start embedding cultural sensitivity into your business? Let's break it down into a detailed 7-day action plan:

- **Day 1: Research and Reflect on Cultural Norms**: Dedicate the day to diving deep into the cultural norms of the markets you're engaging with or planning to enter. Are there specific customs or protocols that are essential to understanding your clients better? What are their typical ways of expressing trust? Spend time researching local greetings, business practices, and even social norms to ensure you don't misstep when interacting with potential clients.

- **Day 2: Analyze and Adjust Your Communication Style:** Think about your current communication style. Are you being direct in cultures that value subtlety? Or perhaps too indirect in regions that favor straightforward dialogue? Today, focus on how you can tweak your language, tone, and communication methods to better align with the preferences of your international clients. If you're unsure, reach out to colleagues or consultants familiar with that culture to get feedback on your current approach.

- **Day 3: Evaluate Your Marketing Campaigns:** Take a critical look at your marketing materials. Do they reflect cultural sensitivity, or are they generic, one-size-fits-all campaigns? Today's task is to adapt your messages to better resonate with your audience in different regions. Consider the imagery, slogans, and messaging to ensure they align with local values and avoid potential misinterpretations. How would a potential client feel when seeing your ad—respected, or overlooked?

- **Day 4: Strengthen Ethical and Legal Compliance:** Today, review your company's adherence to local laws and ethical standards. Are you fully compliant with data protection regulations, bribery laws, and fair trade practices? It's one thing to meet legal requirements but another to actively communicate your ethical standards to clients. Use this day to assess areas where you can improve your transparency and build trust by demonstrating your commitment to responsible business practices.

- **Day 5: Foster Internal Cultural Sensitivity:** To successfully build trust in global markets, your entire team needs to be on the same page. Today, focus on creating or enhancing training programs for your team on cultural sensitivity. How well does your team understand the regions they're working in? Equip them with the knowledge they need to communicate and engage effectively with clients from different backgrounds, ensuring that your company as a whole reflects the values of cultural understanding.

- **Day 6: Personalize Your Approach to Building Relationships:** Think about the specific clients you're working with or targeting. Spend today considering how you can personalize your interactions with them in a way that respects their cultural background. Are there local traditions or business practices that you can incorporate into your outreach? If rapport is key in their culture, what steps can you take to build it before pushing forward with the business discussion? Today is about cultivating relationships, rather than just closing deals.

- **Day 7: Assess and Adjust Your Progress:** By the end of the week, it's time to reflect on what you've learned and implemented. Have you started to notice shifts in how your clients respond to your approach? What feedback are you receiving, directly or indirectly? Take this day to evaluate your efforts and identify areas that still need adjustment. Trust-building is an ongoing process, especially in global markets. What changes can you continue to make moving forward?

What's Coming Next?

As you take these steps toward becoming more culturally aware and sensitive in your business dealings, ask yourself: What would happen if your company was seen not just as a provider of great products or services, but as a trusted partner who truly understands the unique needs and values of every region you operate in? The impact could be transformative. When your clients believe that you "get" them on a deeper level, you not only set yourself apart from the competition—you create lasting, loyal relationships that withstand even the toughest market conditions.

Next, we'll shift our focus to the high-stakes world of **trust in sales with high-value clients**. Have you ever wondered what it takes to build lasting relationships with ***high-net-worth*** individuals or ***large organizations?*** These clients operate differently—earning their trust requires more than a good pitch. It's understanding their complex needs and expectations at an even deeper level. What techniques can you use to gain the trust of clients whose business could make or break your sales year? How do you build trust in high-stakes negotiations where the margin for error is slim? Let's explore those next as we uncover strategies to help you succeed in these critical interactions.

Chapter 15: Trust in High-Stakes Sales

"In sales, especially high-stakes sales, your word is your bond. Breaking it can cost you more than just a deal." — Brian Tracy.

When dealing with high-stakes sales, the pressure to perform is immense. But beneath the surface of every high-value transaction lies one simple truth: trust is non-negotiable. Whether you're working with high-net-worth individuals or selling to large corporations, the stakes are too high for anything less than complete confidence in your abilities and integrity. Have you ever noticed how the slightest slip in trust can unravel even the most promising of deals? Successfully building, maintaining, and safeguarding trust becomes crucial when the stakes couldn't be higher.

Building Trust with High-Value Clients and C-Suite Executives

High-net-worth individuals, large organizations, and C-suite executives share a common mindset when it comes to business: they demand precision, excellence, and unwavering reliability. Whether you're working with a wealthy investor or pitching to the C-suite, the expectations are elevated, and any tolerance for risk or uncertainty is minimal. When dealing with these high-stakes clients, you need more than just a great product or service—you need to demonstrate how you fit into their long-term vision, understand their unique challenges, and consistently add value.

For instance, consider when you're tasked with overhauling a major corporation's IT infrastructure. In this scenario, you're not just selling software; you're selling an all-encompassing solution that will impact their operations for years to come. The trust you build with them is more than the reliability and quality of your product; it also includes the reliability and quality of you, as a partner. These clients need to feel secure that you can guide them through the complexities of implementation, troubleshoot challenges, and scale the solution as their needs grow. It's about understanding not just their immediate concerns but anticipating potential hurdles before they arise and offering solutions aligned with their long-term goals.

And this mindset extends perfectly to **C-suite executives**. When you're selling to CEOs, CFOs, or COOs, their perspective is far-reaching. They aren't just focused on an individual product or service—they're thinking about the ripple effects it will have across the entire organization. The key is this: successful people get where they are by making smart, strategic moves. They're playing chess, not checkers. To truly add value as a partner, regardless of your role, you need to think on their level—or even beyond. You need to play chess too. These high-level leaders prioritize strategic fit, risk management, and measurable ROI. For example, a COO isn't concerned with the technical details of the software; they care about how it will streamline operations, cut costs, or improve overall efficiency. A CFO, on the other hand, wants to know how this decision will impact the company's bottom line—will it increase profitability, reduce unnecessary spending, or improve financial health? Each executive brings a different lens to the conversation, and to earn their trust, you need to tailor your approach to their specific concerns.

Let's say you're pitching a data analytics tool to a CEO. Instead of talking about the intricate algorithms or features, you might say, *"This tool will give you real-time insights that allow you to make faster, more informed decisions. In today's competitive market, staying ahead of trends and acting on data quickly can be the difference between leading and following."* You're not selling them just the tool—you're selling them the business outcomes it will enable. People don't buy products; they buy solutions to their problems. That's the conversation that will capture their attention.

The real key to earning the trust of these high-value clients is proving that you're not simply there to close a deal. They want partners, not vendors. High-net-worth individuals and C-suite executives seek long-term relationships with people who are genuinely invested in their success. They need to feel confident that once the contract is signed, you won't disappear. For example, let's say you've just helped a major investor close a deal on luxury properties. It's not enough that the deal went smoothly; they want to know you'll be there when it's time for maintenance, future investments, or when unexpected issues arise. They are trusting you with a significant portion of their portfolio, and they need assurance that you're not just in it for your commission—you're committed to their ongoing success.

Similarly, imagine working with a CEO who is considering a multimillion-dollar investment in your solution. Instead of pushing for the immediate sale, you could shift the conversation: ***"I understand that one of your goals this year is to enter new markets. Our solution won't just meet your needs today—it will scale with you, helping you grow into those markets smoothly."*** This is how you position yourself as a strategic advisor, and less of a salesperson. When C-suite executives see that you're aligned with their broader vision and are offering solutions tailored to their specific business pressures, trust forms naturally.

One effective way to foster this trust is through **proactive communication**. Don't wait for problems to arise—reach out regularly to check in and ensure everything is running smoothly. For example, if you're managing a project for a large organization, give your clients regular updates on progress, address any concerns early, and show them that you're thinking ahead. This approach is particularly important with high-value clients because it demonstrates that their success is at the forefront of your mind, not the transaction.

And when it comes to **C-suite executives**, don't let the power dynamics intimidate you. Yes, they make decisions that can shape the future of entire organizations, but at their core, they want trusted partners who can help them achieve their goals. They are looking for someone who brings value beyond the immediate product—someone who offers insights, understands their market, and helps navigate the complexities of business at the highest level.

Building these relationships also requires a personal touch. High-net-worth clients and senior executives value professionalism but also appreciate working with someone who genuinely understands their world. Take the time to learn about their industry, their challenges, and even their personal interests. For example, during a conversation with a CEO, bringing up a recent trend in sustainability might open up a deeper discussion, showing that you're not only in tune with their business needs but also aware of what matters to them on a broader scale. It's these small, thoughtful touches that can turn a business relationship into a trusted partnership.

At the end of the day, earning the trust of high-value clients and C-suite executives is about demonstrating that you're committed to their success in a way that extends far beyond the sale. By positioning yourself as an expert, a problem-solver, and a partner who is invested in their long-term goals, you can build the kind of trust that doesn't just close deals but fosters enduring business relationships.

Handling High-Risk Transactions

Navigating high-risk deals is a test of trust at every turn. When the stakes are high, transparency becomes your most valuable tool. Clients involved in high-risk transactions are already on edge—they know that the success or failure of the deal could have significant consequences. What they want more than anything is to feel reassured that you've not only thought of everything but that you'll be honest with them every step of the way. Imagine being in a situation where a multi-million dollar deal is on the table, and the pressure to deliver is immense. The client isn't just evaluating your product or service—they're assessing your character, honesty, and ability to handle challenges as they arise.

In this kind of scenario, being upfront about potential risks, costs, and timelines establishes credibility from the outset. For example, let's say you're in charge of a massive construction project for a client who is investing millions into a new commercial property. Instead of simply focusing on the benefits, you also walk them through possible delays, supply chain issues, or unexpected costs that could arise. You discuss the backup plans you've put in place and the contingencies you've accounted for. When you're this transparent, the client sees you more than a salesperson—they see you as someone who has their best interests at heart, someone they can rely on even when things don't go as planned.

Handling high-risk transactions also means preparing for worst-case scenarios. Clients want to know that you're not relying on a wish and a prayer that everything goes smoothly—they need to trust that you've anticipated the challenges and are ready to deal with them effectively. For example, imagine you're closing a deal on a high-tech software system for a major company. The implementation of this software could impact their entire business, and failure could mean millions lost. Instead of glossing over potential integration problems, you take the time to explain how you've prepared for various outcomes, including potential bugs or delays in the rollout. When you sell your solution, you need to sell peace of mind with it. When clients see that you've thought of everything, their trust in you deepens.

One essential principle to keep in mind is this: *under promise and over deliver*. It's tempting to paint the rosiest picture possible when trying to close a high-stakes deal. But doing so can backfire quickly if any issues arise that you didn't disclose. Imagine promising a flawless, on-time delivery of a new product, only for manufacturing delays to push the deadline back. Now, not only have you missed the deadline, but you've also damaged the client's trust in you. On the other hand, if you manage expectations realistically from the start—acknowledging potential delays while providing solutions for mitigating them—the client will appreciate your honesty and professionalism. Then, if you deliver early or exceed their expectations, you've reinforced that trust even further.

Trust either solidifies or shatters in high-risk transactions. The more honest and proactive you are, the more your clients will view you as a reliable partner who can handle pressure, navigate challenges, and keep their best interests at the forefront.

Trust When the Stakes Are High

High-stakes sales are about managing expectations, navigating pressure, and most importantly, maintaining trust when things don't go as planned. In these situations, clients are watching every move you make—are you transparent when challenges arise? Do you handle unexpected obstacles with composure? The way you respond in these moments becomes the litmus test for your trustworthiness. Think about it: Have you ever found yourself in a high-pressure situation where everything was on the line? How did you manage to not only deliver but keep your client's trust intact?

In high-stakes sales, clients don't just want to hear that everything is under control; they want to feel it. It's easy to keep trust intact when everything is going smoothly, but what happens when there's a sudden obstacle? For example, imagine you're managing a $5 million contract for a new technology rollout for a client's entire business. Midway through the project, you hit a snag—one of the key components is delayed by a month due to a supply chain issue. You could try to buy time and hope it resolves, or you could do what builds trust: immediately inform your client, explain the problem, and offer a plan to keep the project on track. When problems arise, finding the solution shouldn't be your only focus. Continue to be transparent and show that the client can trust you even when things get tough.

The key to navigating these moments successfully is consistency. When clients put millions of dollars on the line, they need to know you are dependable, not only when it's convenient but all of the time. Consistency in communication, delivery, and follow-through are what keep that trust alive when the pressure is on. For instance, consider a scenario where you're handling a high-stakes contract negotiation with a major corporate client. They've invested heavily in your solution, and the timeline is tight. Your team hits an unexpected challenge that could potentially delay the project by weeks. If you've been consistent in updating them throughout the process, when this issue arises, they're more likely to trust that you'll handle it. But if this is the first time they're hearing about a delay, that trust is at risk of crumbling.

Think about it: when was the last time you worked under pressure, and how did you manage to keep trust intact while delivering results? High-stakes sales are a constant balancing act, requiring not just skill but a deep sense of trustworthiness in every interaction.

Chapter Takeaways

Trust isn't a one-time achievement in high-stakes sales; it's a continuous process that you build and nurture with each interaction. Whether you're engaging with high-net-worth individuals, managing risky transactions, or collaborating with C-suite executives, every step you take either strengthens or weakens that trust. The stakes are undeniably high, but trust is the essential element that keeps these intricate deals intact. You've explored the importance of transparency, honesty, and consistency—not as mere concepts, but as the core values that form the bedrock of successful relationships in high-stakes environments.

You might have noticed that these principles of trust-building remain consistent, regardless of the situation. While it may seem more intense when you're navigating larger, more complex sales landscapes, the fundamentals stay the same. By sticking to the basics—being transparent, delivering on promises, and communicating often, and honestly—you'll find that these practices are just as effective, no matter the scale. Trust is a universal currency; the same approach that works in smaller, everyday interactions can lead to great success even when the stakes are at their highest. Whether it's a major deal or a simple negotiation, staying grounded in these principles ensures that you'll build lasting, meaningful relationships and achieve consistent success in any trust-building opportunity that comes your way.

7-Day Trust-Building Action Plan

- **Day 1: Reassess Your First Impressions**
  Evaluate how you present yourself to high-value clients. Does your initial contact convey trustworthiness? Consider how you can refine your opening conversations or proposals to immediately establish credibility and transparency.

- **Day 2: Strengthen Your Expertise**
  Dedicate time today to deepening your understanding of the high-value client market or a specific client's business. Read industry reports, study client challenges, and prepare to present yourself as a more informed, trustworthy advisor.

- **Day 3: Review Your Communication Methods**
  Analyze the clarity and honesty of your client communications. Are you being transparent about potential risks or overpromising on deliverables? Make adjustments where necessary to ensure that you are setting realistic expectations that build trust.

- **Day 4: Anticipate Obstacles in High-Risk Deals**
  Create a list of potential challenges in your high-stakes deals. How will you address these risks with your clients? Proactively bring up these risks in your next conversation, showing that you're prepared and unwavering even when things don't go according to plan.

- **Day 5: Engage with a C-Level Mindset**
  Prepare a pitch or presentation aimed at a C-suite executive. Focus on how your solution ties into strategic goals like risk reduction or ROI. Reframe your value proposition to match the mindset of a top-level decision-maker.

- **Day 6: Underpromise, Overdeliver**
  Evaluate your current deals and adjust any promises or timelines to ensure you'll exceed client expectations. Make this a regular habit to build trust by delivering more than what was expected.

- **Day 7: Become a Trusted Advisor**
  Reflect on how you can position yourself more as an advisor and less as a salesperson. Reach out to a client with advice or insight that doesn't directly relate to a current deal, but adds value to their business. This establishes long-term trust.

Now, as we wrap up this part of our discussion, it leads us naturally to an important question: What happens when markets are disrupted? How does trust come into play when the landscape shifts and uncertainty rises? That's what we'll explore next—**Trust in Market Disruption**. When industries are upended and change becomes the only constant, trust becomes more than a competitive advantage; it becomes your lifeline. Let's explore how to build and maintain trust when everything around you is changing.

Chapter 16: Trust in Market Disruption

"Disruption is an opportunity to earn trust by showing your customers that you can adapt and still deliver." — Gary Vaynerchuk.

In times of market disruption, the pressure on businesses can feel overwhelming. But have you ever noticed how these challenging moments also serve as an opportunity to build deeper trust? When industries shift—whether due to technological advancements, new market entrants, or economic changes—companies are forced to adapt. How you manage these transitions speaks volumes about your reliability. Clients are watching closely, wondering, "Can you still deliver when the game changes?" In moments like these, trust becomes the cornerstone that helps you not only survive but thrive in an unpredictable landscape. When you prove that you're capable of adapting without compromising your values or the quality of your service, you cement a level of trust that can outlast even the biggest disruptions.

Building Trust Amid Industry Disruption

Disruption often feels like chaos, but it's also an opportunity. Think about major shifts in industries like retail, where brick-and-mortar stores faced competition from e-commerce giants like Amazon. Many traditional retailers struggled to keep up, but those that survived—like Walmart—adapted by building robust online platforms, investing in technology, and demonstrating their ability to change with the times. Customers trusted that even as the landscape shifted, these companies could still meet their needs.

Another prime example is the automotive industry. With electric vehicles emerging as a major market disruptor, traditional automakers like Ford and General Motors had to pivot quickly to remain competitive. They not only have switched their focus to building electric cars; they doubled down on communicating their long-term vision and commitment to sustainability. This earned the trust of environmentally-conscious customers who might have initially leaned towards Tesla but were now seeing these legacy brands embrace change without losing sight of their core values.

When faced with disruption, it's not enough to simply adapt—you need to do so in a way that reassures your clients. They need to see that while the industry may be changing, your ability to meet their needs remains constant. Whether it's shifting to remote work models in a post-pandemic world or integrating AI to streamline operations, the key is to communicate how these changes benefit your customers and strengthen your relationship with them.

Transparency During Disruption

When markets shift, it's tempting to downplay the potential challenges in an effort to maintain confidence. However, one of the quickest ways to lose trust during a disruption is by failing to be transparent. Clients would rather hear the honest truth about how a new market entrant or technological advancement might impact your services than be left in the dark.

Imagine you're a software company facing an unexpected regulatory change that could delay product launches. If you remain silent, clients may speculate, assuming the worst. But if you communicate upfront—explaining the potential delays, how you're addressing them, and what steps you're taking to mitigate disruption—you maintain their trust even when things aren't going perfectly. Clients appreciate transparency because it shows that you value their partnership enough to be upfront, even when the news isn't ideal.

Consider Netflix when they first announced price hikes and shifts in subscription plans. Initially, the lack of clear communication led to customer frustration and loss of subscribers. Netflix learned from this, and later disruptions—like changes in content distribution or new platform features—were handled more transparently. They went further than simply announcing the changes; they explained why these adjustments were necessary for the company's long-term vision and how it would ultimately improve the customer experience. This shift toward greater openness helped Netflix regain trust.

Being transparent doesn't mean oversharing every little detail, but it does mean providing clarity on the changes that matter most to your clients. They should never be left guessing about what's happening behind the scenes.

Resilience and Trust

In the midst of market disruption, resilience becomes one of your greatest assets. Demonstrating resilience—whether as a company or an individual—reinforces trust because you illustrate a response that is thought out and strategic rather than an impulsive reaction. Clients need to see that you're not crumbling under pressure, but are instead standing firm, prepared to face any challenges alongside them.

Think about the global pandemic and how it tested the resilience of nearly every business. Some companies, like Zoom, quickly became household names because they were able to adapt to the sudden surge in demand for virtual communication. Zoom didn't just meet the immediate need for video conferencing—they continuously improved their platform to accommodate a massive influx of users. Doing so reassured customers that they could handle the pressure and continue delivering a reliable service.

On a smaller scale, consider a local restaurant that shifted to a delivery-only model during lockdowns. By being flexible and resilient, they were able to maintain customer trust even when their traditional business model was no longer viable. In addition to surviving, they were able to show their customers that no matter what challenges arose, they would still find a way to deliver.

Resilience goes beyond surviving disruption; it's about thriving in it by demonstrating to clients that you're prepared, adaptable, and always focused on their needs.

Chapter Takeaways

Trust during times of market disruption is not built on perfection, but on transparency, resilience, and the ability to adapt while maintaining core values. Customers and clients are looking for honesty when things change. They want to know that, despite the disruptions, you're still committed to delivering value. This isn't about hiding challenges or pretending everything is business as usual—it's about being open about what's happening and how you plan to move forward.

Now is the time to reflect: How do you handle disruption in your business? Are you proactively communicating with your clients when changes happen, or do you wait until they ask? Think about the last time you faced a market shift—how transparent were you in your communication? How resilient was your business in responding to unexpected changes?

Here's a 7-day action plan to help you implement the lessons from this chapter:

1. **Day 1: Reflect on Previous Disruptions**
   Look back at a previous industry disruption that impacted your business. What worked well in your response? What could have been done better? Write down the lessons learned.

2. **Day 2: Identify Current or Potential Disruptions**
   Review your current market and identify any potential disruptions on the horizon. Is there a new competitor, technology, or regulatory change? List out how these changes might affect your business.

3. **Day 3: Communicate with Your Team**
   Set up a meeting with your team to discuss how you'll handle potential disruptions. Encourage open dialogue about risks, solutions, and how to maintain transparency with clients.

4. **Day 4: Draft a Transparency Plan**
   Create a template for communicating any disruptions with your clients. Be sure to include a section on how these changes will ultimately benefit them despite the challenges.

5. **Day 5: Build Resilience into Your Operations**
   Identify areas in your business where you can strengthen resilience. This could be improving your supply chain, enhancing customer support, or investing in technology that allows you to pivot quickly when needed.

6. **Day 6: Reach Out to Clients**
   Contact a few of your key clients and ask for their feedback

on how they feel your business has handled disruptions in the past. Use this feedback to refine your approach.

7. **Day 7: Implement Changes**
   Based on your reflections, team discussions, and client feedback, make the necessary adjustments. Whether you're improving communication transparency or operational resilience, put your new plan into action.

By following this plan, you'll not only be better prepared for future disruptions but also deepen your clients' trust in your ability to adapt and thrive, no matter what challenges come your way.

Conclusion

Congratulations! You've made it to the final stretch, and I want to take a moment to truly acknowledge the journey you've been on. Trust is no small thing—it's the glue that holds every meaningful relationship together, both personally and professionally. Throughout this book, we've uncovered the many layers of trust, peeling them back to reveal how essential it is in every aspect of your sales journey, your brand, and even in navigating the unpredictable waves of market disruption.

Think back for a moment. How has trust shaped your own experiences, whether in a business deal or in a personal relationship? Meeting someone you can trust feels like an instant connection, one that deepens over time through actions rather than words. It's the same in sales. Clients don't just want products or services; they want to believe in the person or company they're dealing with. They want to know they can count on you, not just today but also in the future.

Remember the *Trust Equation* we explored earlier? Trust isn't a mysterious, unattainable quality. It's something you actively build, one interaction at a time, through credibility, reliability, intimacy, and keeping your focus on your clients' needs. Every single client interaction is an opportunity to strengthen those bonds, to show up authentically, and to listen with intent. And if you've been paying close attention, you'll know that *active listening* is one of the most powerful ways to build trust. When you truly hear what your clients are saying—beyond the words—they feel valued. They feel like their needs are your priority. And that's how trust becomes unshakable.

But trust goes far beyond the one-on-one relationships. It's building a *trusted brand* that people believe in, even before they meet you personally. We talked about how social media plays a crucial role in this. Your online presence is often the first place people encounter your brand. So, ask yourself: Is your brand communicating the values that matter most? Are you being transparent, authentic, and engaging in ways that resonate with your audience? Social media goes beyond broadcasting—it's really about creating trust on a much deeper and more expansive level, even if that's through a screen.

And then there are the challenges that come with *trust amidst disruption*. Let's face it: the business world is constantly changing. Whether its new technology, market shifts, or increased competition, things can get uncertain fast. But here's the thing—disruption doesn't have to erode trust. In fact, it's in those challenging moments when trust is tested and solidified like a broken bone. Will you be upfront about the difficulties or hide behind excuses? Will you reassure your clients through transparency or leave them in the dark? It's these moments of uncertainty that can make or break your reputation. I've found that being open, even about the risks, builds more trust than simply glossing over the tough stuff.

Building and maintaining trust isn't all about grand gestures; it's the daily, intentional choices you make that create a lasting impact. Here are some everyday actions you can take to reinforce what you've learned and to keep trust at the core of everything you do:

- **Check in with yourself each morning.** Reflect on whether your actions align with your values and the promises you've made. Trust starts with being true to yourself.

- **Listen more than you speak.** In every conversation, focus on understanding the other person's perspective. Make sure your clients feel truly heard.

- **Always follow through.** Whether it's a small task or a major project, keeping your commitments consistently strengthens your reputation.

- **Be proactive in communicating challenges.** When something isn't going as planned, address it head-on. Clients appreciate transparency more than excuses.

- **Engage meaningfully on social media.** Instead of just posting, start conversations, respond to comments, and show that there's a real person behind your brand.

- **Ensure that your brand reflects your values.** From your marketing to your client interactions, make sure everything you do is a reflection of the integrity you want to project.

- **Anticipate client needs.** Look ahead and offer solutions before issues arise. Clients will trust you more when they feel like you're thinking ahead for them.

- **Be consistent in how you show up.** Trust is built through steady, reliable actions. Make sure that no matter the situation, your clients know they can count on you.

- **Ask for feedback regularly.** Don't wait until something goes wrong. Proactively ask your clients how you're doing and where you can improve.

- **Celebrate your clients' successes.** When your clients win, take the time to acknowledge it. Show them that you're as invested in their growth as your own.

As you carry these actions into your daily life, you'll find that trust isn't just a concept; it's a living, breathing part of everything you do. It's the bedrock upon which all your professional and personal relationships are built.

Before I leave you with one final thought, I'd like to ask for a little favor. If this book has helped you, inspired you, or even just made you think about trust in a new way, I'd love to hear your thoughts. Your ***"positive review feedback"*** on Amazon Kindle will help other readers discover this book and allow me to continue sharing these insights with more people. It's a small act that will mean the world to me, and I'd be incredibly grateful for your support.

So, as you go out into the world and apply what you've learned, remember this: Trust is the currency of all successful relationships. It's what sets you apart, opens doors, and keeps people coming back. Keep building it, nurturing it, and living it, and the rewards will come—both in business and in life.

Thank you for taking this journey with me, and I'm excited to see the incredible things you'll achieve by putting trust at the center of everything you do.

--Dean Thacker